The
Golden Thread
More Teachings from White Feather

Given through the mediumship of
Robert Goodwin

16/7/07

16/7/07

with love and light

Amanda & Robert

The Golden Thread

First published 1999
This reprint 2005

ISBN 0 9535210 0 1

Other books by the same author(s)

Truth From the White Brotherhood
Robert Goodwin
Available from Psychic Press, The Coach House
Stansted Hall, Stansted, Essex CM24 8UD

Answers for an Enquiring Mind
Robert Goodwin & Amanda Terrado

In the presence of White Feather
Robert & Amanda Goodwin

Available from R.A. Associates
Suite 62 Beacon Buildings, Leighswood Road
Aldridge, Walsall, West Midlands WS9 8AA

Visit the White Feather website:
http://web.ukonline.co.uk/mandrob
Email: mandrob@ukonline.co.uk
whitefeather@bluecom.net

Cover design: Dolphin Associates/Phil Jeyes
Front cover photograph by Photodisc
Printed in the UK

Published by R. A. Associates

This book is dedicated to all those souls who have helped me along my spiritual pathway, both upon this earth and in the spirit world. I thank you for allowing me the privilege of your friendship.

With love to Mom & Dad,
Amanda and Nicki

There is a Golden Thread
that runs throughout all of creation,
without it nothing would exist.
It's name is Love.

CONTENTS

*Readers should be aware that White Feather's
teachings are exclusively oral and the contents of
this book have been transcribed from recordings
of his philosophy.
Wherever possible the text remains true to the
spoken word despite some inevitable repetition
and only punctuation has been added in the
interests of continuity.*

Foreword

I write, having had the privilege of knowing both White Feather and the medium through whom he speaks. It is a great honour to have been asked to write the foreword to this enlightening book 'The Golden Thread' having thoroughly enjoyed 'Truth from the White Brotherhood', Robert Goodwin's first book of spiritual teachings.

I know that both Robert and White Feather, his guide, are fully committed to bringing spiritual truths to the attention of as many souls as possible in order that we might all find some comfort and be inspired to enhance our individual journey towards spiritual fulfilment.

Neither man would take credit for the enormous amount of time and effort needed to pass on these great teachings but having been closely involved I can tell you that a great deal of love and many hours of communication have gone into this work. It is an ongoing task that will hopefully bring forth further enlightening philosophy.

In this world of materialistic ventures, selfishness and greed, this book is like a breath of fresh air, raising our thoughts to a world beyond, where we can be assured of a better life. If only a portion of these teachings touch your heart it will have served its purpose. Let us read and inwardly digest the work of two truly spiritual men.

A.L.S

Introduction

As a thinker and seeker of truth, I cannot help but reflect upon the many achievements of mankind, particularly during my own current lifetime. His advances in the fields of scientific study, medicine, the arts, communications and such like are staggering.

And yet, there still exists so much ignorance about 'life after death', with the two seemingly opposing viewpoints of mainstream science, with it's atheistic stance and orthodox religion, with it's 'follow the Son of God and be saved' scenario, both of which I totally and utterly reject. God existed long before science and religion were even thought of. In fact, were it not for God, then neither could ever have been thought of. For God is within us all and our own freewill allows us to think, reason and believe whatever we choose.

My own reasoning mind has enabled me to move from ignorance towards something of an understanding of the true nature of existence. I was born a medium and came upon this earth as many before me, to help bring enlightenment to those who would listen. In this great task I have been extremely privileged to work with a man whose words you are about to read, and our two-world partnership, stretching back now over twenty five years has been both a delight and a revelation to me.

Despite my many faults, I have always been given the opportunity to maintain my links with the spirit dimension and to have been able to help so many people by allowing myself to be used as a channel for guidance and truth has given me great compensation for all that life has thrown at me. I have much to learn, both of life and of myself. But this much I know to be true; there is no death. If you believe nothing else, believe this. Quite recently a close friend said to me 'If life after death is a fact, why isn't it known by all?' The fact is, you DO know, but because of the nature of physical incarnation, you have merely forgotten from whence you came.

More and more people are awakening to the fact that life is infinite and eternal. Mediumship is proving so each and every day in Spiritualist centres throughout the world.

Of you the reader, I ask only this; read the words of White Feather with an open mind. They are his words and his teachings, not mine. But I believe them to be true, for I know that they originate from a more evolved soul than I and they are given, in love, to help and assist you and all of humanity towards a greater realisation of life.

Do not waste the wonderful opportunity that you have to discover these truths. They belong to you all.

Robert Goodwin
January 1999

Chapter One

The Discerning Mind

The power to discern right from wrong is one of the most important aspects of human behaviour. Here White Feather speaks of the need to venture beyond the five physical senses and to link with the higher self and it's greater abilities:

" Now this aspect of discernment is a critical one and one about which I intend to speak to you briefly tonight. For it is an important lesson which every soul, particularly those engaged upon the spiritual undertaking of service, have to contend. For your earth is a plane of illusion. The life which you lead is, by and large, an illusion. It feeds the senses with information which is often distorted and incomplete and inferior. Those who have no knowledge of the inner dimensions of existence rely almost exclusively on what their five senses tell them. But you who have begun to awaken your higher states of being know that much which is presented to you is only a part of the truth, and indeed much of what is presented to you is inaccurate and untrue. Nevertheless, all too often those in your world are unable to discern at critical moments and to sift out that which is true from that which is untrue. Sometimes this is useful to the soul because it can be utilised in such a way that it enables the soul to learn a lesson. For every mistake that you make, every time you stumble and fall, there is a lesson to be extracted, something to be learned. But there has to come a time when your higher critical faculties begin to 'lock in' and begin to register upon your consciousness. What we are speaking of goes beyond the five senses. We are speaking of the gifts and the abilities of the soul to see, to understand,

and to register that which is. There are those in my world - and I am sure that you in your world have encountered such souls - who, when you meet, look you in the eye and KNOW. It is as if, when they look at you, they see right into your being and know you for what you are. To them you are transparent. You can hide nothing. Whatever sham you may exhibit to others, whatever mask you wear, whatever face you adorn, you cannot in any way fool such individuals. This quality is one which I would urge you to develop and unfold. It is a quality of the soul. It is that which has to be earned, like all the gifts of the spirit, but one which once recognised and brought into play will enable you to see more clearly and to understand, and to base your decisions, your actions and even your words and thoughts on a certainty, because you KNOW without doubt.

You may say 'But White Feather, how do we obtain this state of being?' Like all the gifts of the spirit and anything which is worthwhile, each must obtain it in their own way and their own time, but always at the expense of attributes which we should say are akin to the physical level. In other words, you must increase your sensitivity at the expense of that which would deny your sensitivity. You have to work, you have to unfold, and you can only do this through a careful process of sitting in meditation, of opening yourself up to the spirit, of sensitising yourself to those subtle energies of the spirit. To do this requires discipline. It also requires patience and sacrifice. This is why I say it is at the expense of some of the things of the world of matter which you enjoy and which take up your time. But let me reassure you that every sacrifice that is made in this direction will reap a multitude of benefits. Because the increased sensitivity of your being, even though it may lead to some distress in the sense that you also are able to register the anguish and pain of your world - that is a price you have to pay - is worthwhile.

When you look at others, look into them. Put yourself into their heart, into their mind, into their soul, and see them. Not for what they say they are, or for what they are believed or perceived to be, but for what they truly are.

Discern their being. You can only do this, as I have said, through discipline, through practice, though sacrifice. But it is a most valuable gift. It is priceless, it cannot be measured. It is a true gift, a true quality of the soul."

On a separate occasion the guide spoke of the need for each mind to reach out beyond its earthly limitations and of the great beauty that awaits it:

"The mind, despite its limitations, or those imposed upon it by the form through which it expresses itself, is capable of infinite beauty and grace. It's true greatness and magnitude cannot be comprehended by mortal man. But so often we find that, embodied through the human form, the mind is almost dormant, akin to that of a sleep state. Of course, it can never be still, but it does not truly reach out to explore the great ocean of infinite knowledge that surrounds it. Instead, it seems to spend a great deal of its time on things of a temporal nature. Like a child playing with toys it dabbles with understanding. It grasps at straws as it tries to evaluate the purpose of life and the reason for being.

Often it is only when it is touched by sorrow, by trauma, by difficulty, that its latent divinity begins to express itself and for the first time it begins to think and to explore deep within the chasm of its being, where, to its surprise it finds new depths of understanding. For it is within, that the great truth of life is cradled."

The wise spirit sage often refers to the wisdom that lies at the heart of every soul and of the need to rise above the lower aspects of life which prevent us from gaining access to it. Here, he speaks in typically fluent fashion of what he refers to as 'the battleground of the earth' before delivering some words of great comfort to all engaged upon the pathway of spiritual discovery:

" There are many in your world who seek enlightenment, who seek truth in far distant lands, in great temples or within the recesses of books, or by listening to learned tongues. But you know, the answers lie within you. When you look within you then you find the great reservoir of true spiritual energy. The true 'power of the spirit' lies within you.

You are here upon the battleground of earth to eradicate weakness, disharmony and discord. To challenge accepted beliefs, orthodox creeds and dogmas, to rise above the lower mental states of being that would hold you back and imprison you to this cycle of birth and death. It is difficult I know, because the lower mental states are powerful. But when you begin to attune to your higher soul you become aware of your weaknesses as your strengths are revealed to you. You become aware of the darkness within as the light of the higher mind shines.

These are difficult times for you. Times of confusion, of heartache, despair. But these are times to rejoice because you are truly becoming aware of the power within and are beginning to harmonise with it. It can never be easy. If it were, then all upon your world would be elevated in a short space of time to the status of liberated souls. That is not the purpose. You have to learn through darkness, through toil, through difficulty. When everything seems to be pulling you down, when your body fails you, when your heart is heavy, when your soul cries out.

I look within each of you and I see your own private battles that you have with yourselves. But I rejoice at this, because I know that you will emerge victorious because it is the will of the spirit that you should. Never forget for one moment that you are beings of light. Your very essence is of light. You may walk in the shadow and you may think that all around you is darkness and despair, but YOU are light.

When man learns to observe his bodies of himself, he will see that they are of light. Each body has its frequency and its colour. Every organ has its colour and its vibration and man is a glowing sphere of light. Your thoughts are light. The very breath which you inhale and exhale is of light. You are a galaxy with myriad points of light throughout your being. Man looks out into the universe through his telescopes and sees the many stars and planets in the universe. But when he learns to look into the inner universe he will see a wondrous galaxy stretching far into the depths of his being. It is filled with light.

The power to transform *you* is within you. The power to transcend lower mental states to reach the heights of enlightenment is within your grasp. Never forget that you are linked with the highest soul in my world. There is a river that runs from he who is enlightened, who stands upon the mountain top, to the one who toils away in the valley below. That river, that winds down, is called love. It is love that binds us all together.

I speak to you in this manner tonight because, like you, I have walked upon the earth. I know the pains and the trouble that you feel, but it is encouraging for you and helpful for you to know that you are not alone. That the burden which you carry, you do not bear alone. We are always by your side, even though we cannot and would not endeavour to take that burden from you because we know that to do so would hinder you. It does not mean that we do not sympathise with you and have compassion for you, but we see not with the blinkered eyes of humanity, but with the eyes of the spirit and with a little of the wisdom of the spirit that sees not merely today or tomorrow, but all that lies ahead of you and beyond. All of that which you cannot see because you are not permitted. We see the glory that lies ahead of you. We see the radiant beings that you truly are. We see the latent divinity that is within you awaiting to express itself, to burst forth into the glory of radiant light - and we rejoice.

Always hold fast to that which you know to be true. Always give of your best. Always endeavour to be right. Always have kindness and sympathy in your heart, gentleness in your touch, compassion in your words and love in your hearts, for these are the qualities that endure into eternity. For they are 'the power of the spirit'.

Chapter Two

The Aura and the Energies of Life

At one gathering of a development group White Feather commenced his talk with his usual customary greeting to all present and then proceeded to speak, firstly about the energy fields which surround all of creation and then about ways in which we, as humans could help ourselves by avoiding some of the man made 'pollutants' which can affect them:

" May I greet you all with the divine love and the radiant light of the Great Spirit. I am pleased to have this opportunity to link with you again and to come into the orbit of your thoughts and aspirations. It fills my heart with joy to be able to share with you in this communication, the great love, truth, light and wisdom of the Great Spirit. For as I have said many times; it is ultimately truth that is the liberator of souls.

I am aware of your desire to unfold the latent divinity within you and also of your dedication, your persistence and the various attributes of your higher self which seek to be made manifest in your lives, and it is good that you should endeavour to unfold the beauty within you in this way, because the rewards are beyond description.

I want to give you a teaching tonight regarding the various energy fields that surround you, which are commonly referred to as the aura and the auric fields. There is little understood in your world of these energies and it should not be thought merely that the aura is a reflection just of the physical well-being, because it is much more than that. To commence, you should understand that you have many levels of being; physical, etheric, astral, mental, spiritual. All of these coerce and inter-penetrate in accordance with their varying levels of vibrational energy and each level has its own energy field surrounding it. So when you are fortunate enough to see what you term 'an auric field', you are seeing, frequently, not just one level but many levels, many fields. For the auric field is composed of many, many levels of energy.

Every facet of your being is surrounded by energy. In fact your whole state of being is energy. But what is termed the auric field is a reflection of the state, frequency and vibrational level of energy that surrounds that particular level of being.

Every organ in your body has its own energy field surrounding it. Your heart, your lungs, your kidneys, every facet, every part of you has its own colour, vibration and sound. These things are aspects of each other and should not be separated, but recognised as different expressions of one energy. Naturally, wherever you see a vibrancy of colour it indicates, more often than not, a healthy organ or a healthy state of mind or emotional being, and conversely where you see the dull, muddy colours of the aura, it indicates a state of disharmony or disease or imbalance. But of course you must learn to read these colours, you must learn to understand. Just as you have to learn to understand everything that is unfamiliar, and this only comes by observation, by attunement, by raising your own vibrational energies to the point where you can not only see these energy fields but also come into harmony with them, to understand them.

The auric fields around you are also a protection, a barrier if you like, against undesirable energies. When I link with this instrument, just as when your guides and helpers link with you, it is necessary to enter into this energy field that surrounds you. This is why frequently you will experience an expansion, as if you are gaining in size and dimension. To me, the aura of the instrument through whom I speak is my prison when I am working through him. For I have to confine myself to its walls and dimensions, to its energies. Just as I have to confine my language to that which is known by his conscious and unconscious levels of being. So it places great limitations on what I can bring through. But that is the case with all forms of mediumship, when we have to work through an instrument who is encased within a physical form.

There is a great deal of nonsense talked about the aura! As there indeed is, upon your world, concerning many aspects of spiritual knowledge. I have heard it said for example, that an individual has a 'torn aura'. How can this be? Is it to be thought that the auric field is a fabric? Or a cloth that can be severed? What the individual is sensing, either through their clairvoyant vision or by the mere fact that they have attuned with the energy level of that individual, is a depletion in one area of the auric field, perhaps through one of many causes. It may be an emotional drainage, a physical disease or a mental condition or state of mind. Because just as your auric field expands in your meditation, when you are happy and when you strive to reach to the higher plateau of understanding, so it contracts when you are sad, when you are down, when you are ill. When you are perhaps tired, when you are emotionally depleted. It contracts to the point where it is very close to the physical body. So you must understand that the energy field, in its varying levels, is a creation of you as an individual.

You can think of it if you like as an extension of you. Your body does not end at the periphery of your skin. It continues beyond that. Why do you think it is, that when you come into the presence of one or other, that you are able to sense something of their nature? Perhaps something of their past history or something that lies in their future, recognising that beyond your world, in the higher realms, past, present and future exist in a different sense than they do in your linear time. It is because you are sensing it in the aura. Because it has to be said after all, that you are all instruments of the spirit in degree, and in accordance with your unfoldment so you can sense many, many things."

At this juncture the guide went on to suggest some procedures that individuals could implement in order to help themselves when their energy levels became depleted:

" When you are depleted, tune in to your own self. Tune in to the energy that surrounds you and you will find that with practice, like all things, you will become more highly sensitive to your needs. If for example, you are lacking in physical energy, then you can imbibe the energy that will give you strength and upliftment. It may be the vibrant red with its wonderful strong vibrancy, or the verdant green that is of nature. For you are familiar I am sure, that when you are in nature surrounded by valleys and hills and trees and flowers, that it gives you an upliftment. This is not merely a psychological upliftment, it is because you are breathing in and imbibing the energies of nature. You see, you do this naturally, unconsciously, without any conscious will. But to do it as an application of will, is a wonderful thing and it should be practiced, in my view, by each of you on a daily basis.

You must understand also, that your auric field can become polluted and tainted by many things around you. By the interaction with other beings, also by the very atmosphere in which you have your being here upon the earth. For man pollutes his world in many, many ways. Chemically, electrically, he poisons the air, he taints the water, he soils his own nest, he soils his own bed. And you have to move and have your being within this. Would that you would take the time to cleanse your auric field by immersing yourself in water, preferably of a cool or cold nature, of drying your body and then of taking in deep breaths. Of imbibing the healing rays of the spirit. Would that you would take frequent exercise and that you would be mindful of the food and drink which you imbibe, for these also have their aura and are containing of great energies.

You know, some in your world pay more attention to the oil that they put in their motor engines than the food that they consume. They pay more attention to their television than they do to the matter that they ingest through conversation, through reading, through thinking. All of these things are either pollutants or stimulants, or else they provide a gentle balance. You move and have your being within a sea of energies. You are constantly giving forth and receiving.

You are aware, are you not, of how one can drain you, whilst another can uplift you? You are aware perhaps, as you have found to your delight this evening by holding a gentle creature in your arms, you can receive great healing and great love. On the other hand you are aware, are you not, that another such creature can instill fear into your heart when he surprises you?"

[Here, the guide was referring with some humour to an incident with a cat and a mouse, which had previously caused some alarm to one of the group]

"These things have an effect upon you. But to still the mind. to quieten the body, to rest the weary limb, to calm the heart, to bring the thoughts into a state of focus, these things are good for you. Remember that you are what you create. You are today, what you thought and did and said and believed yesterday. And you will be tomorrow, exactly that which you are creating today. But the auric fields that surround you are energies of great beauty. They can provide for you many, many things. They can ensure that there is balance and harmony and wholeness and health between all the levels of your being or they can be indicators that there is, at one level or another, some imbalance within that needs to be addressed.

So perhaps in your moments of reflection you can think upon this teaching and it will provide for you some further guidance that will assist you along your pathway of unfoldment."

This teaching provoked great interest within the group and many of those present were eager to ask further questions of the spirit mentor:

Q: "You often speak of 'new energies' coming in to our earth plane, could these energies have a disruptive effect upon us or are they of a benign nature?"

White Feather: "The energy itself is of a benign nature. The disruption that can occur is not caused directly by the energy but by the effect that it may impart around you, to which you are sensitive. The energy itself is one that brings an increased sensitivity and so you are thus more aware of the distinction between the higher and the lower. Do you understand that?"

Sitter: "Yes."

White Feather: "That is as succinctly as I can put it. It is rather like a wind that blows and as it does so, the leaves upon the tree shake and vibrate. A few, fall. Some simply respond in their vibration. The wind in itself is not good or bad, it just IS. But all the leaves upon the tree have to respond in one way or another. Some are unable to withstand the wind that blows and so they fall by the wayside. Others, because their attachment is strong and healthy and because they have an allegiance to the power and the energy field of the tree, find that there is an upliftment. Do you understand the simile?"

Sitter: "Yes I do. May I also ask another question which concerns those of us who, at times may feel unwell and find that the particular condition which troubles us does not seem to lift or respond to treatment. Could this be due to Karmic law or some other reason? Can you comment upon this please?"

White Feather: "I do not intend to speak of individuals, but you must recognise that when a condition does not yield for whatever reason, then there may be other factors which have to be taken into consideration.

The Karmic aspect is certainly one of them. Another, is the ongoing situation regarding the current existence upon the earth, the many aspects that may combine within that situation regarding lifestyles and in particular, thinking and emotional levels of being. Also of course, there is the point that all discomfort and suffering, if it is of a deeper, extended nature, may have been chosen by the soul level of that individual to undergo in order to learn a particular lesson and until the soul is touched, until the lesson is learned, then the condition will not clear. It will not lift, despite whatever attempts are made to clear it. So you have to look at all these aspects. You have to weigh up and consider that which may be apparent. All that you can do as individuals is to give of your best, to try your hardest.

But let me say this; that when you truly know yourself, when you are truly in touch with the higher principles and where you allow those principles to express themselves fully in your lives then you will find that there can be no disharmony. You will find that health will be achieved, within the limits of natural law. Naturally, a limb which has been removed or an organ which has been taken out cannot be replaced. But where it is within the operation of natural law, there you will find that balance and health and wholeness must return, because it is the law that it should. If it persists in a state of imbalance it proves only one thing; that at some level of your being you have not yet achieved that level of harmony and thus you are in contention with the operation of the law. Do you understand that?

Where there is perfect harmony of thought, of emotion, of action, there the law is in harmony with you and you are in harmony with the law, and health and wholeness and oneness must be the result. It can be nothing else."

Q: "Can I ask a question about all the violence and suffering and pain and hurt around us, all that is going on in the world......how does this affect us? What effect does all the negative energy around us have upon us? I find it so difficult. Should we respond in a certain way when those around us cause us pain? How does it all affect us?"

White Feather: "It depends upon you as individuals. But let me say that ignorance breeds ignorance, darkness breeds darkness, evil breeds evil. But it depends upon each individual. You can have one who is surrounded, in the midst of ignorance and darkness and yet they do not allow it to touch them. It is difficult I know, because as I said earlier, you move within an ocean of these thoughts and energies and emotions and words and deeds.

You as individuals have to learn to separate the light from the dark, the good from the bad, the wheat from the chaff. You have to learn to extract the gold from the ore. Sometimes it requires that you go into the lion's den in order to do that, just as the miner must go into the bowels of the earth in the darkness and the dirt, in order to find the gold that lies within. That is sometimes very necessary. But where you have knowledge, as you have a little - as you each have a little - where there is awareness, there you will find there comes a strength and fortitude that accompanies it. There also comes a responsibility, for you cannot have increased knowledge and sensitivity without responsibility.

What you need to do is to trust yourself. Trust that responsibility. Trust the power of the spirit that has never let you down, that has never deserted you, that has never abandoned you. That has always awaited within to hear your call. And you will find always that the compass of the soul, which is the higher self, will speak to you and guide you correctly."

Sitter: "Could I ask another question regarding development of spiritual gifts and of being able to see the aura and other aspects of a person. Is there anything that we can do to help ourselves?"

White Feather: "You can help yourselves by learning to attune. Now, when we speak of 'seeing' the aura, remember that there are many ways of seeing. You can 'see' with your eyes closed, just by looking with your inner vision, and that is attunement. It is necessary to increase your sensitivity by sitting in a disciplined manner to unfold the gifts that you have within you and the more often, the more frequently you can do this, the more regularly you can sit and the more that you can place yourselves in a position of harmony and attunement, not only with your higher self, but with those that are drawn to you out of the magnetic attraction of love, you will find that so you become more honed, more polished, like a diamond that has been polished and that radiates perfectly and reflects perfectly the light of the spirit that shines upon it. Then you will see."

At this point the guide asked all of the sitters to look at his medium as he informed them of his intentions:

White Feather: "Look, and you will see an aura, because I am going to project an aura of my own into the aura that surrounds him. Look and you will see or you will sense a colour. And you can all do this and perhaps you can compare notes! Some of course, will be able to partake of this exercise more easily than others, but that only proves to demonstrate the case in question. I shall be interested to hear your comments afterwards for I shall remain in your midst for a little while."

After wishing the group a fond farewell, the spirit teacher slowly relinquished his control of his medium and the meeting was brought to its conclusion. However, it is interesting to note that in the normal discussion that took place afterwards the medium had no recollection of what White Feather had said in his reference to the 'experiment' of asking each sitter to view the aura. It was not until, after some ten minutes of conversation, when one of the group suggested that each of the members 'compare notes' of what they had each seen that the medium, with some incredulity, commented "What are you referring to?"
When it was pointed out that the guide had asked the sitters to look and see the medium's aura, it was quite obvious to everyone that he had no

recollection of this being spoken through him. It may be of interest to note that, although some of the group saw nothing, several did report a blue-green light around the medium which is evidence that the teacher did indeed keep his promise.

Chapter Three

Service - the Passport of the Soul

During his many public and private discourses, White Feather often speaks of 'service' to the Great Spirit and humanity as being one of the major attributes of a spiritually developing soul. Allied to love, it is evident that service is a powerful tool which not only assists in helping those who are in need but also enriches the giver beyond measure. Here, during a talk given to members of a development circle, he outlines the need to serve in whatever way possible:

" We bring our love and blessings from the spirit dimension. It is written that 'many are called but few are chosen'. It is with these words that I address all who come within the orbit of this teaching. For there are many of you, who because you have reached that point in your spiritual unfoldment where the gifts that lie buried deep within you can be brought to the surface, are beginning to awaken to the great reality that you can be recipients of truth and partakers in this great plan that is forever unfolding and that encompasses every facet of creation.

There are many who are beginning to recognise the great potential that lies, almost dormant within them. There are many who are realising that they are the possessors of psychic and spiritual faculties that await activation so that they may be used in the service of the Great Spirit through helping mankind reach forward beyond the material dimension and into the spiritual.

Very often those coming into this state of awareness need guidance and help, need patience and understanding and love shown to them, because they are not always aware of the changes taking place within them that result in the opening up of their being to a higher faculty of awareness. Those of you who have already awakened the spirit potential should endeavour to shed light upon those who follow in your footsteps. To help them as you were helped. To guide them as you were guided. To inspire them as you were inspired. I wish I could say that the awakening of a spirit faculty was the answer to all of life's problems, but alas it cannot be. It may seem a great paradox but nevertheless it is a fact that the one who serves and who is served by the spirit must himself, first have been touched deep within. Perhaps by pain or fear, or worry or anxiety. Or by whatever difficulty was necessary for the gifts lying within to be brought to the surface.

I am frequently asked by those seeking to use their gifts and arouse their higher consciousness, 'What are the qualities needed to be a servant unto this great truth that seeks to express itself?' which brings me to that of which I spoke upon the commencement of this talk - 'many are called but few are chosen'. In truth, all have a divine potential within them, because you are all parts of the Great Spirit.

Because you are all facets of that great mind, you all have that mind within you. Thus, you have perfection - be it latent perfection, within you. Potentially you are all mediums, you are all psychics, you are all seers and you are most certainly all servants of the Great Spirit. But not all can be recipients of this higher teaching at this moment in time because they are not yet ready. You have perhaps heard me say before that 'when the pupil is ready, the master appears'. When the fruit is ripe it can be picked, not until.

Those who are engaged as channels for this great benign power to flow are chosen because they are ready for this work. Because at some point or at some stage they have been touched by the hand of the spirit and the divine spark has been kindled deep within them. Each must have the assets that can be used in service. These are; patience, love, tolerance, control of the emotions - particularly the lower emotional states - and an inner drive and a yearning to be of service and to impart this great truth that is the divine inheritance of each man. Love is perhaps the greatest of these attributes. For love is a great force in the universe. Love, in its highest and purest state embraces all facets of creation. Nothing and no-one can be excluded from this. Love seeks nothing for itself, only that it can fulfil itself by embracing you and by passing from you in its embrace of others. For love, in its highest and purest form cannot be selfish or blind in any form. True love is beyond all boundaries and all barriers. True love cannot be confined to colour, race, religion or form. For true love recognises all of creation as being part of a oneness and a unity that has at its centre the Great White Spirit.

Patience and tolerance are aspects of love. They recognise, again, a oneness between all of creation. Those of you who are tolerant of others' weaknesses, are so because you recognise those same weaknesses somewhere within yourselves. Those who see the efforts of others in striving to throw off the chains and shackles that physical life imposes upon the spirit, recognise that same fight and that same struggle within themselves. And thus it is because they have been touched in this way, they have struggled, they have fought, they have overcome, that understanding has come to them. And when they see in others the same inner promptings that they themselves have had, then they have tolerance towards their fellow man.

Control over the emotions is an essential part of any aspirant to service. For if one cannot control one's own mind then one certainly cannot be an instrument for other minds to control. It is essential that one who aspires to serve the spirit gains control over the emotions and learns to find stillness within the self, learns to place the mind into a state of receptivity where, although it is placid, it is alert. Where, although it is still, it moves."

Paying particular attention to those seeking to develop as mediums the spirit orator highlighted the fact that it is not always those who are in the spotlight, who are necessarily the greatest servants of the spirit:

" All too often developing mediums rush into this or that phase of activity. Their spirit is keen, their heart is willing, but they are not yet ripe as channels through which this great power can flow. Control over the self is therefore essential, an essential part of being a servant of the Great Spirit. But let me say this; service encompasses many fields, many spheres of work and activity. I have been speaking primarily of those who are what you call mediums. But service encompasses all aspects upon all levels. There are many in your world who are not what you call mediums but who are nevertheless channels for the spirit. There are many who do not recognise that the spirit uses them. There are, for example, many doctors and surgeons who do not realise that their hands are guided by the hands of the spirit doctor and the spirit surgeon. There are many gardeners who tend to their flowers and their trees without realising that they have unseen helpers guiding them and prompting them. There are those who labour in the fields, who toil in the workplace and yet are not well read, do not have letters after their name, do not speak upon any platform or work within any sanctuary or subscribe to any church or any religion, yet they are servants to the spirit.

Each has his part to play. Each has his role, his place and his time. For in truth, all are servants of the Great Spirit in some way or another. As I have said many times, we do not look upon you and judge. We do not compare one against another and say that one soul is greater than another or better than another. For we see in all men, the children of the Great Spirit. We see in each of you the same divine spark that lies within ourselves. In some it is but a tiny flicker. In others it is a great roaring flame that emits warmth and light, that embraces many who are drawn to it like moths to a candle. That divine spark that is within all can never be extinguished. Even in the lowest of the low it is still there.

All too often it takes pain and suffering, hardship, disease, anguish and death before it can be awakened. But ultimately, all are on the same pathway, without exception and without exclusion, because all are parts of the Great Spirit.

Those of you then, who would seek to quicken your vibrations, who would seek to open your hearts and your minds to this great fountain of light should always aspire to the very best within yourselves. Do not accept second best. Do not accept that you are ever defeated. Do not let anything or anyone be your master, but seek always to be master of yourself and your own destiny.

Learn to unfold the gifts of the spirit, which I have said, and repeat again are; love, tolerance, understanding, compassion, patience, kindness. Learn to control your mind, your thoughts and most importantly your emotions, and learn to release your mind from its self inflicted prison, that it can explore for itself the inner realms of light and find therein the truth and the reality of which we speak.

Never doubt that you are spirit first and foremost. Put fear out of your mind because fear saps, erodes, drains and removes the vitality that the spirit gives to you. Close the door to fear. Close the door to all that holds you back, that ties and binds you, shackles and chains you. Do not adhere to any of the creedalism or dogmatism, ritualism. Do not march in the procession of ceremony that seems to be instilled in the minds of those who aspire to be religious. We are not interested in religion. We are not interested in the singing of hymns or the reciting of prayers unless they come from within the being, from within the heart's centre.

Much that is uttered in the name of God is devoid of any real essence of truth and purpose. Your churches, and I speak now of your orthodox religion, are like empty shells that enclose a vacuum. You who are the aspirants of truth do not need these edifices that have been erected and are still being erected, where the Great Spirit can be worshipped. You have your own temple. You have your own place. You have your own shrine and your own sanctuary that lies deep within your own being. Is it not better to enter into this temple that you may speak with the Great Spirit and He with you? So these are my words to you who aspire to serve the Great Spirit. Go forward with renewed optimism and hope. With renewed strength and vitality. Cultivate those things of which I have spoken and seek always to serve whenever the time is right and the opportunity presents itself. For every effort that you make is met with a greater effort in my world.

No one who earnestly desires to serve, to bring a little light and truth into the world, is alone. You draw unto yourselves a gathering band of liberated souls whose one desire is to serve you and to serve the Great Spirit, which is the common link which binds you all together.

May the blessings of the divine mind enfold you with their love and their tenderness until the next time."

On a separate occasion when speaking upon the subject of service, White Feather spoke at greater length about the nature and purpose of mediumship and its role in providing hope and comfort to those in need:

" Firstly let me say that mediums are not created, they are born. Their constitution, which enables the flow of spirit and psychic energies to be made manifest in your world, is one that is conceived entirely through natural means. The gifts with which each instrument is endowed can be nurtured, can be cultivated, can be developed, can be brought to the surface so that they may be utilised by those in my world that are the manipulators of the various degrees of spirit energy, but they must be there in the first instance. They cannot be created by man. I know that there are those who would disagree with this, but I maintain that it is a truism that cannot be altered.

The purpose of mediumship is divine. Its directive is firstly to provide a link between the seen and the unseen, or between the higher and the lower states of being. Put another way, quite simply to create a bridge between the spirit world and the earth world, across which can flow communication in all its various connotation and formulation. Be it healing, be it thought energy, or communication, inspiration or revelation. For mediumship embraces a vast panorama through which all manner of manifestation occurs. When this link has been established, provided the individual adheres to what his inner self directs, this link cannot be broken.

There are those who say that the prime directive of mediumship is to prove the continuance of life beyond the point of death. I would not disagree with that, but I would add that this is only a small part of its work. For such is the nature of the link that is established between minds that have a common bond between them, there is a great deal more that, if it is allowed to do so, can be brought into your world. Knowledge, wisdom, guidance and inspiration, healing and an inner revealing of the true purpose of life in all its multitudinous forms.

Man is a creature of ignorance, but he must move ultimately from ignorance into knowledge, from darkness into light. And he must come, ultimately into an understanding of the fundamental realities of his existence. He does not terminate with the death of the physical body. He continues in an unbroken sequence that sees him advance from ignorance into wisdom and from the outermost to the innermost. Those of you who are aspiring mediums must realise that yours is a sacred gift bestowed upon you by the Great Spirit. Not by chance, but because you have earned the right to receive it.

Mediumship is a faculty of the etheric and physical constitution, but also of the mental and spiritual constitution of the individual. When the two embrace, a channel is formed through which the power of the spirit can flow. You who are sensitive should always aspire to the highest and best within yourselves, trying at all times to live in accordance with the divinity that strives to express itself through you. Purity of thought, of speech and of action are paramount in enabling the sensitivity of the individual to be refined. Grossness of any kind, adherence to lower thoughts and emotions all detract from the sensitivity and cause the spirit energies that seek to communicate to waver when they reach your aura. You should always retain an ambience of humility at all times, to strive to serve your fellow man, to help those who are burdened, to comfort those who are ill at ease, who are stricken with disease or disharmony, who are anxious or worried. To provide a light in the darkness of those whose lives are filled with despair and misery.

Realise that mediumship carries with it a great responsibility, not only to the self but to those whom you seek to serve. You have a responsibility to the Great Spirit. You have a responsibility to the self to try and always provide a clear channel through which the spirit can work and you have a responsibility to others in ensuring that you do not mislead or misguide.

Mediumship is a pathway that provides the aspirant with an opportunity to partake and participate in the great plan of life that is at work, but by its nature means that the sensitivity must be increased. It is a lonely pathway, it is a difficult pathway. It is one that is sometimes filled with pain, for as a man becomes more sensitive to the subtle energies of the spirit, so he also becomes more sensitive to the pain and suffering of the earth plane that is all around him. This is where you must be disciplined and strong and forthright. You must be like the tree that has its roots firmly planted in the soil of knowledge. Not as the leaf that trembles and shakes with every passing breeze. For when the wind blows and the storm clouds gather, the leaf is blown from the tree and swept away, but the tree remains steadfast and firm and is immovable."

Continuing the theme of mediumistic development the teacher spoke of the conflicting views that existed concerning the type of mind best suited to being employed by spirit guides:

" There are those in your world and also in mine who are of the opinion that a medium should not be equipped with knowledge for fear that this hinders the mind that tries to work through it. I am not of this school of thought for I believe that the more knowledge a mind has, the more that the spirit can utilise that knowledge to its own ends and ultimately interface with it so that it may be brought through the instrument to serve mankind. There are very few mediums today who are taken under complete control by their guides.

It is a mental process that is activated for we must blend our auras with yours. We must blend our minds with yours and seek to gain access and control of the subconscious mind before impinging our thoughts through the consciousness. A blank mind is an impossibility, but a mind that is ignorant can impose a formidable barrier. Where there is knowledge, avenues are formed along which we can project our thoughts and control can be established and maintained, in my opinion, more easily. We can then direct our thought energies along these pathways and even though they may become a little 'coloured' by your own thoughts, the essence of our teachings can be brought through."

White Feather then went on to once more emphasise the need to put fear out of the mind and to embrace the power of love in all that we do:

"Above all, control your fear and self doubt. When you sit in your meditation open your hearts as well as your minds. Know that the link that is established is forged, not only by the power of attraction, not only by friendship, but by love. Love is the great force, the great underlying energy and power behind all things. It is essential that you have love in your heart, that you aspire to greater things and that you seek to serve not yourself, but humanity and the Great Spirit.

Those who seek to serve themselves do not progress. They do not unfold their spiritual gifts. Mediumship is a vocation and like Spiritualism, is a way of life. There are very few TRUE mediums in your world. There are many who think they are mediums, but who are not. There is a great deal of psychism that passes as mediumship, but psychic energies operate in a different way and can do so without the spirit world being touched. All of you who aspire to be mediums should seek and call upon the power of the spirit, not merely the power of the psyche.

You may say 'How do we know the difference? How can we tell?' I would answer 'You will know'. If you are sincere, if you are honest, if you are true to yourself, you will know when the spirit speaks to you, when the hand of God touches you. It is unmistakable, but you must experience it for yourselves.

Mediumship has a divine roll to play in the furtherance of truth and knowledge throughout the universe and within your world. It is a sacred institution and its members are blessed because they serve the light that seeks to serve them. You cannot put any measure upon the work of the medium. You cannot say that service, in its varying degrees is high or low, because you carry not the yardstick by which you can measure it. In our book there is no high or low service. There is but service. As I have said before, it is not always the one who stands upon the platform, who works within the spotlight, who receives the applause and the plaudits, who is the greatest servant. There are those who sit in silence, who work within the sanctuary, within the circle, within the group. There are those who work within the factory, at the office, in the field, who are servants of the Great Spirit. There are the healers, there are the counsellors, there are the listeners. There are those who say nothing and yet give out love, who radiate light and kindness and benevolence to all who come within their orbit. These are the servants of the Great Spirit."

Chapter Four

Where there is Spirit, there is Life

The question of when life actually begins, is one which has puzzled mankind for centuries and many minds have debated over when individual existence commences. Some believe that the 'soul' joins with the foetus in the womb. Others, that it does so at the moment of birth. Whilst still others maintain that it links at the moment of conception. Here, the learned spirit teacher explains what actually transpires when incarnation takes place:

"Very often you know, I am asked the question, 'Where does life begin, and where does it end?' Let me say firstly that I know nothing of beginnings or endings when we speak of life. I know only of that which is infinite. Because all is in essence part of the Great Spirit, nothing is in any way segregated from the Great Spirit, from that great divine mind of light and love and intelligence that devised the boundless universe with its multitude and myriad of forms from the most complex to the most simple.

You have always existed and you will always exist, because there is no beginning and no ending. Life is truly infinite. And yet, there is what I call a commencement or indeed, many commencements upon different avenues, different pathways, that lead into many areas which challenge, which provoke change and which enable the soul or the spirit to reveal its inner-most divinity. Such a commencement occurs when you enter into a physical existence, a physical incarnation into this of your earth plane. But when does the spirit enter that? When does life as you understand it in the physical sense, begin? Now you know there are many views on this. Even in my world there are differing opinions, but as I have said many times; where there is spirit, there is life, where there is life, there is spirit. I maintain that at the moment of conception, when the male and the female halves link through an act of love, then there is life. Where there is a division of cells, there is the spirit within that, and despite some who believe that the soul or the spirit links with the form at some later point I must refute this and say categorically, and to repeat myself; that where there is life, there is spirit, and where there is spirit, there is life.

However, there are many levels of linking with that form because the lesser cannot contain the greater and it is that in that tiny spark of life, even though an individualised spirit has linked with it, there still is not facilitated an absolute link that enables the thinking, reasoning processes that you now enjoy. Because that tiny form has not developed its physical apparatus. It does have its brain and its nervous system and all the other various components that enable the spirit to manifest through a physical body and register its consciousness upon your earth plane. But that is why there is a period of nine of your months to enable the foetus to develop within the womb of its mother and as this occurs, an etheric matrix is created to which the physical body conforms.

Certain genetic factors which are inherited through what your scientists have described to you as the genes, determine physical characteristics such as gender, height, build, weight, colouring and certain hereditary dispositions, certain hereditary gifts and predispositions to certain weaknesses and disease, perhaps later in life. This is programmed into the physical apparatus. But linking with that, is the spirit. The individual mind which has chosen - if it has earned the right to do that - it has chosen that vehicle as the vehicle that enables it to gain expression and experience upon this world. Now there are various stages which you are aware of, particularly those of you who have borne children, where there is a quickening that takes place within you and you feel the movement. That is one aspect that facilitates a greater linking with the incarnating mind and spirit and its physical counterpart. The greatest of course, is at the moment of birth when there is entry into your world and that soul, which has chosen that vehicle through which to experience, takes its first breath upon your world and begins to awaken its five senses that enable it to take in so much information as it passes through its life.

Even through its infancy, even as it is growing up there is still a greater link being obtained. This is why your children, because they do not have yet, the physical apparatus, in brain and nervous system growth to facilitate the full expression of the mind, are still naive and innocent in their outlook. They do not sense danger as you do. They have not, the knowledge or the wherewithal or the wisdom to know always what they are entering into. Even so, within them there is the aspect of conscience which tells them within, what is right and wrong, even though at times they are not consciously aware of it. But gradually, the soul begins to express itself and when this point which you call puberty is reached, there is a further quickening, and you find that the greater depths of your children become evident.

You are aware of a deepening of character are you not? Of an emotional aspect? Sometimes this expresses itself in many strange and wonderful ways. Sometimes it is in the form of a rebellion. At other times it is in an awareness, where a child will begin to question why and where, begin to look and examine for itself what awaits it in life. To begin to find, through its first tender steps, its way and its progress that lies ahead of it. And when that child reaches the age of around twenty-one - we cannot be directly distinct about this because these are not hard and fast rules you must understand, but general terms of which I speak, because the spirit does not confine itself to the measurement of years and time as you do - but when it reaches this point there is facilitated perhaps, a completion of that cycle and the fully mature individual is able to link, the mind and the emotions are able to link, with your world. Of course, there is some flexibility in this because there are some of that age who are still spiritually and emotionally immature, whilst there are others who are fully mature. You see what I mean by this of the spirit compared to the measurement of your time?

What I am trying to explain to you is that when the spirit links with the body, it is a slow and gradual process and that continues until that point is reached where all of the faculties; emotional, spiritual, mental, physical, can coerce to a degree where you have a fully individualised spirit who can gain experience through the many vicissitudes of life. The many experiences, this polarity of light and dark, negative and positive. This spectrum of life through which it passes. And this is the purpose of life. It is to give you experience.

You do not learn when all is sunshine and light, when all is a bed of roses, when all is going well. If you look back through your lives you will find that the greatest lessons were obtained in difficulty, in trauma, in heartache. When your innermost latent divinity was called upon to express itself and you were able to find that inner spark, that inner revelation that enabled you to conquer a particular situation. If you do not conquer that situation, then in all probability, through the law that operates, of which you are all a part, it will present itself again, perhaps at a further point in this life or even perhaps at a future point in another life. But you must understand that you have to go through this.

It is, I know at times very difficult for you. I have stood and watched. I have stood at your grave-sides, I have seen the tears come down from your eyes. I have watched at times as you have struggled and have had to stand back as many who love you have had to stand back, because we are not allowed always to interfere in that which is soul growth. But we do so always with love and with compassion because we know that, that through which you are passing is ultimately that which will liberate you. Which will bring you into the light of understanding and there is nothing else that you can do that will enable that to happen. You have to pass through it. You have to understand it. And it is to be hoped that through this, your journey of life, you equip yourselves for that which is to come. When that life span is completed, then the point is reached which you call death. A word which I do not like to use but which I use because you are familiar with it. Death occurs when the connection between the lower and higher aspects which is obtained and maintained through what you understand perhaps as the silver cord, that spiritual umbilical that joins your lower with your higher, when that is severed, death occurs. And each of you will continue to exist in an unbroken sequence regardless of your beliefs, regardless of your understanding, regardless of anything, because you are spirit.

You do not acquire a spirit body at death. Neither do you enter into the spirit world, although this is a term which is often used. You are already in the spirit world. You already possess a spirit body. All that happens is that the heavy grossness of the physical form falls away to enable the wondrous spirit within to continue to express itself. And that is the purpose of life; to come, to touch upon the earth, like a stone sent skimming across the waters of life. At times you touch upon experiences, at times you move from one to another, but in reality it is only when you sink to the bottom, when you sink and rest and find peace and the stillness that lies within the depths of experience that you come into true knowledge and true awareness. That is greater than anything that I can put into words.

As I look out upon you I can see that you are all at different levels of being. Some of you have both feet upon the spiritual pathway, some of you have one foot, some of you but dip a toe into the water of life. But you are all upon the same pathway. All that I would say to you, and I have said this many times to many souls is; to endeavour to give of your best. To do of that which you believe to be right regardless of what others may think of you or say to you. If you know that it is true, then adhere to it. Because always the truth will win through. Nothing can prevent it from doing so."

At this juncture the spirit guide invited questions from the gathering to whom he was speaking. As ever, his response to the questions asked was both interesting and thought provoking:

Q: "I want to ask, that as we have a physical body and it contains a spirit, is there a universal plan as to when that cord breaks?"

White Feather: "Let me say first of all that the physical body, in reality, does not contain the spirit. Rather, the spirit contains the physical. It is the spirit that is master, it is matter that is servant. It is the spirit, which is the greater, that contains the body of matter, which is the lesser. As to the point of separation, that is dependent upon many factors, not least of which is the free will that operates within each of you, the conditions into which you manifest and the way that you conduct yourselves in your interaction with others around you and indeed with all of life. So there are many factors here which have to be taken into consideration. However, let me state that when the time which you call death occurs, there is nothing that anyone in your world can do - no doctors or scientists.....anyone....healers or whatever - can do to prevent that passing taking place. Because when that time is reached, it is the law that operates with its usual mathematical precision and the silver cord is separated gently and the two bodies drift apart. When death occurs, there is no turning back. There are no miracles in that sense. You cannot return once that separation has been made. Do you understand that? Does it answer your question?"

Sitter: "Yes."

Q: "At the moment of conception how is the spirit of that particular life form chosen?"

White Feather: "Again, it depends upon the individual. Let me say that sometimes there is not a choice. It is an automatic operation of the law, but where through successive lifetimes of experience the soul has equipped itself with the necessary knowledge and has earned the right to choose that into which it incarnates, then it exercises that right from a soul level. It is the soul, the highest point within you that chooses, in its infinite wisdom, the vessel into which you are about to incarnate. It does that, taking into consideration all the various imponderables and the many factors which are involved, including parentage, line of descent, environmental and social conditions, because it knows that, that particular mix and blend will enable it to have the greatest possible experiences that are necessary for that particular facet to grow and to expand and to be polished until it shines in the light of wisdom. Do you understand that?"

Sitter: "Yes, thank you very much."

The next questioner appeared to have opposing views on the guide's statement that the spirit joins with the body at the moment of conception. Here White Feather first answers the initial question and then, having evoked a further response from the person concerned, who still appeared to be at odds with the guide, further emphasised the way in which the law operates regardless of individual belief:

Q: "I find it difficult to accept that life begins on conception. I think that in our earthly area there would be many complications with people believing that that is so!"

White Feather: "I am not concerned, I am not interested what people believe in that sense......only that they believe the truth. If they wish to believe something else, that is their prerogative. I cannot alter the facts and the law. You perhaps heard what I said when I stated that in fact, life exists before conception. Conception is only a commencement. It is only a commencement on a particular pathway of an individual that has its own personality that is distinct from the individuality that enters into it. But I maintain that it links with that at the moment of conception. Now the reason why many will find that difficult is because there is an epidemic in your world of abortions. Of those who seek to destroy the physical body before it has had a chance to ripen and to gain entry into your world. Those who undertake this in ignorance must pay a price. Those who undertake it in knowledge and understanding must pay an even greater price because the law operates perfectly, and simply by removing a physical form in your world it does not deny the spirit from progressing and unfolding and developing into that individual in my world. Let me say that there will be many in your world who, when they pass into the spirit realms, when their physical body drops away and they continue to exist, will face up to many souls whom they did not even recognise had existed, and that will be a great shock to them. Do you understand the point I am making?"

Sitter: "No, not really I don't."

White Feather: "What is your difficulty?"

Sitter: "Well, the difficulty is that you only spoke of abortion, I never mentioned abortion."

White Feather: "That is true."

Sitter: "I am speaking of births....there are difficult births....births where there are complications, still births.....and a few more too."

White Feather: "Absolutely, absolutely. The law is still the same. Son, the law is still the same. It does not matter whether it is an abortion, whether it is a still birth, whether that soul touches your world but for a few moments or whatever, the law is still the same. Where there is a link made at conception, there you have an individualised spirit. I am sorry if you cannot accept that but I cannot change the law to please you. It is a fact and that is the law."

At this point the debate moved in other directions, but it was evident to all present that the spirit sage, whilst always inviting of debate and respectful of others views and opinions, was also totally forthright and uncompromising regarding his views on the operation of natural law. The reader, whilst free to decide, may wish to reflect on the fact that many spirit children return, communicating through mediums to prove their continued existence following death. It must be remembered that 'death' can occur both before and after 'birth'. Souls who have experienced a passing by means of a still birth, an abortion or other birth related complications do not simply cease to be, or even cease to have been initially. Were this the case, then it would make a mockery of personal responsibility and would evoke great sadness for those who would be expecting to meet their 'unborn' child when they themselves passed into the spirit world at death. It is a sad reflection of the world in which we live that many souls have little or no knowledge of a life beyond this earth and that the souls of many children whom they believe to have not even come into being, are in fact watching over them with great patience and love. As the guide says; the law is the law, and even though man may take what meanings please him, the truth is eternal.

Chapter Five

The Spirit Dimension

Speaking here about the spirit world, White Feather firstly refers to the various 'planes' or levels of existence into which we pass, before elaborating further on other aspects of life beyond the earth plane, including what is termed 'the second death':

" You see, there are a great many minds in my world as there are in your world. In your world they exist on one plane, on one level. The good and the bad, the knowledgeable and the ignorant, the fruitful and those whose motive is to serve only their own interests. In my world that is not the case, for minds dwell in the sphere to which they are accustomed through their own thoughts and endeavours. I have heard it spoken that there are seven levels in my world, of ascension. I would like to know who discovered this and who has found it to be fact because I have yet to meet anyone who has reached the highest level, who has ascended to the summit of all knowledge and wisdom, illumination and light. What you must understand, and this may come as a little surprise to you, is that these levels of being have not been created for the minds that inhabit them. Rather it is, that the minds which inhabit them, create them. Do you understand that?

Now this applies not only to the higher levels of the spirit world but also to the lower levels of the spirit world and also to your earth plane which I consider to be also a level of the spirit world, albeit a physical expression. You see, if you think about it the world which you live in, is a world which man is shaping and creating by his thoughts and his actions. Now you may say ' How can this be, when there are trees and mountains and rivers, streams and valleys, birds, fish and insects that were created long before man appeared upon the earth. They were created by the same mind that created humanity, but humanity has been blessed with freewill, which the lower levels of being do not enjoy and when freewill comes into operation then it begins to create, it begins to formulate, it begins to change and your world of matter is slowly changing and conforming to the thoughts of the collective consciousness.

You see, you are already reaping the results of wrong thinking upon your earth. You are reaping the results of pollution of the air, of the oceans, of the soil. Many of your species of animal creatures which provide great comfort to humanity are vanishing from your earth. This is a result, not merely of actions but of the thoughts behind those actions. Because thought is the father to the deed.

In my world, the higher principle world, thought is not merely subjective, it is objective. You see, let me explain that a little more clearly. When you think a thought it is subjective in that it cannot be seen in normal circumstances by others in your world, unless they have the gift of insight, and it only becomes apparent when it is externalised through words or through actions, do you see? In my world, that is not the case, for when you think a thought, even though it is subjective, it quickly becomes objective. It is externalised, it can be seen and the results of it are far more powerful and instant.

Those in the lower planes of my world, the dark realms as they are termed, are there as a result of their thoughts and their actions. Those levels of being would not exist if there were not the minds to populate them. They would not exist. You heard me say, did you not, when I last spoke to you, that I have to employ the use of the astral body to communicate. I have to leave a portion of my consciousness in that form. If I did not do so then it would dissolve, it would cease to exist. It is the same with any level in my world. If there is not the thought form to create the level, to justify the level, then it ceases to be, because it serves no purpose. Nothing is wasted in my world.

There is no waste, everything is as a result of the energy of thought that creates and manipulates and formulates all substance.

You may wonder then, to what level will you ascend when you finally discard the physical body at the point of death? It is not my intention to speak to you individually on this matter but I would say that those who have sought honestly, through their endeavours to serve the spirit or to live their lives in service to their brother, who have tried to do their best and their utmost, whose motive is to be good and to be kind, will generally, pass to what I term or what is termed 'The Summerland'. And this will be in order to express through the astral body, a body which you have as I speak. It is not something you acquire, you have it already. To exist upon that plane, now that is a plane that is very akin to your world, only much more beautiful. We have the rivers and streams, the birds and fish, the flowers, all the creatures of your kingdom. It is a place of simple and yet profound beauty. But you do not remain here, because as wondrous and as beautiful as this place is, it is only a stepping stone to greater soul growth and expansion and there occurs what I would refer to as 'the second death'.

Now, I know that the mere mention of the word 'death' strikes terror into the hearts of some! But it is nothing to fear. Just as the death of the physical body is only a passing moment, so 'the second death' is a similar experience where the soul sloughs off the astral body, unless there is a purpose for maintaining a portion of it, and continues in the spirit body, the higher mental state, to continue its soul growth and progression through the higher realms of the spirit world.

So you see, this is what awaits you and it is a wondrous journey. It is a most exquisite experience when you finally begin to remove the outer layers which hold you back. The denseness, the heaviness, the grossness of all that is of the lower elements, to reveal within, the pristine beauty of the spirit form. The form that, in its higher aspects is formless. The thoughts that cannot be put into words. The expression that is beyond expression. The truth that is beyond description. These are the beauties and the infinite expression that awaits you all. It is a wondrous, wondrous experience. One which each of you is undertaking as I speak. You think your experiences upon the earth at sometimes are beautiful, when you are able to aspire to reach the heights of greater expression, but I say to you in the greatest respect and the deepest humility, and the most wondrous love for you all, that you but paddle around in the mud.

You see, compared to the true radiant expression of the spirit, your world, despite its beauty, is very crude, very basic. We have all been upon the pathway. I am no exception and I am not in any way greater than you. Just as you are not greater than I. I have been upon your earth. I too, have wondered around in the darkness thinking that I know so much and yet knowing so little. Thinking that I know the truth and yet, but glimpsing the greater reality and purpose of life. It is the path of each soul, none are excluded. But the great truth is that through this there comes the soul expansion and the reaching out to the radiant light of understanding.

I hope that this has been of some import. I try to work within the context of your ability to understand. You must recognise that it is difficult to express the infinite through that which is finite.

I wonder if you have any questions that you would ask of me before I take my leave?"

Speaking about a book she had read in which is described how a building is created in the spirit world by means of thought, a sitter asked the guide if it had ever been possible for man to build in that way upon the earth, perhaps using mind energy to move stones or other obstacles such as in the construction of the pyramids and great temples of the past:

White Feather: "Not in the sense that it is described in your literature, but of course man is always, as I have said, creating through thought either directly or indirectly. Everything that you see around you is as a product of thought, but of course the things of material substance cannot be easily manipulated by the application of mind energy because at this level it is not possible to penetrate the denseness and manipulate form. In my world, because the mind is in harmony with that level of being upon which it exists there is a natural tendency to be able to manipulate matter.

Perhaps I can describe it to you in this way; if you try to move a great boulder by pushing it, you cannot do it. But if you strive to lift a feather then you can do so. Both are material forms of substance but the one is much lighter and more refined than the other. It is a crude metaphor but you see, the more in harmony you are with the form, the easier it is to manipulate. The denser, the heavier, the grosser the form of matter, the more difficult it becomes. Do you understand?"

Sitter: "Yes. The other thing is, I was very curious....there was a chapter on birds and these birds lived in the Summerland and they had a greater understanding than those birds on the earth. I was wondering how this applies with the animals, do they inhabit the Summerland?"

White Feather: "The birds and all the creatures of the earth inhabit the Summerland. Yes, it is the plane which is occupied by all the creatures of your earth. When you say 'understanding', you must understand yourself that creatures do not exhibit the same measure of understanding that is attributable to the human expression because that is not the purpose. But there is, like all aspects of spiritual advancement, a greater expression, a purer, more refined expression in my world than there is in yours simply because the dense physical body precludes, or excludes the pure refined expression of spirit and mind."

Another sitter seemed interested in how we are seemingly able to 'astral travel' into the spirit realms, particularly when we enter into the sleep state:

Q: "You know, sometimes we have a feeling that we don't want to walk somewhere....we could just go....is that a memory in our minds, the fact that we have actually done this.....just thought and gone?"

White Feather: "Yes! You do so each night when you go to sleep and you leave the physical body behind. When you do this, very often you know, you gravitate through your thoughts to where your desire takes you. It is not necessarily that you evolve into the spirit realms. You may stay very close to the earth plane on the astral plane, because this is the nature of desire, but where the higher soul principle is able to express itself then there is a drawing of the individual towards the light, towards the higher self and you may well express yourselves in the spirit realms, particularly upon the Summerland plane of which I have spoken this night. There is some recognition perhaps, when you return to your physical body, be it scanty and fragmented, but that is what you are registering."

At another gathering of the group two weeks later, the spirit guide once again took up the reigns of his previous discourse and continued from where he had left off:

"May I greet you with the divine light of the Great White Spirit. I am privileged to be once more in the midst of such esteemed company! For I know that you and I share the common purpose of endeavouring to unfold the latent divinity of the spirit which is within us, because you see spiritual aspiration and development and unfoldment is not merely common to the earth plane, for it never ceases. Just as you seek to develop your own divine potential so also do I. For life is a constant striving to unfold all of the richness and beauty that lies within. In many ways it is a struggle for the more that one evolves the more that one becomes aware of the inherent traits which may be referred to as weaknesses but which are ultimately recognised as being aspects of the individuality which have to be refined, which have to be, in some respects, eradicated, in others developed and honed and sharpened so that each individual may be like a stone which is polished until every facet is able to shine in the radiant light of truth.

I want to continue my talk on this occasion, from whence I left off. If you recall I was speaking to you about the spirit world in which I dwell and the journey which each soul undertakes when it sloughs off the physical body and finds itself in the spirit body which it has created through its own individual endeavours, through its earthly sojourn.

You will perhaps remember that I spoke of what I term 'the subjective reality', in that everything that occurs is in accordance with the mind, the spirit that creates it. This applies to my world as it does also to yours. You see, in your world the mind operates, as the spirit does, through a denser, grosser form which you know as the physical body. Through that you experience a multitude of expressions; joy, sorrow, laughter, pain, freedom, captivity, darkness, light, negative, positive and your physical body, that wondrous machine which is the product of aeons of evolution that have enabled it to be honed and refined and developed, is able to sense the environment through which it moves and this is transmitted through the nervous system to the brain where it is interpreted by the mind.

You see, always we come back to the mind. Whatever you experience, whether it is joy or sorrow, whether it is laughter or pain, ultimately comes down to the response, the mental and the emotional response. Because without the mental aspect the body is nothing. Without the spirit and the mind the body is dead meat. It has no purpose. Always the mind and spirit have to interpret the signals which move and pass through the body. Now, in my world the aspect of mind is more pronounced. You see, as I have already said to you, each level in my world - and there are many, many levels, is in accordance with the mind and spirit that exist upon that level. If there is not the intention and the purpose and the desire of the minds upon that level, then that level would not exist. It exists because of the individuals and the collective that dwell upon that level.

There are many realms of light and there are many realms of darkness. Because this is the opposite, the law of opposites in operation. I do not want to dwell for too long on the darker levels but I will say to you that I have visited these places. I have been able to do so only because of my experience and because of the resolve which I have developed. No one ever ventures alone into these places. They are always accompanied by what I would term 'an Angel of Light'. One who has a great light and a great knowledge and is a kind of protector. For you see, the minds that dwell on these lower levels are very strong and powerful and it takes a great mind, a strong mind and a strong spirit to resist the power of such minds. Upon such levels dwell minds who have, upon your earth, committed acts of evil, of great selfishness, of hurtfulness, of a diabolical nature and the environment which they create is from their own being. It exudes from their being. They are part of the spirit just as you, for the light, the spark of the divine, is never extinguished. But in such souls it is very dim as to be almost unseen and unrecognised.

Those who have perpetrated acts of pain continue to do so. They themselves, experience the mental aspect of this. Those who have dwelt all their lives building, collecting, storing wealth and possessions find that they are bereft of such 'luxuries' as they would term them. They are bereft of all that they have sought to hold onto often at the expense and the suffering of others.

Each is in accordance with itself. The scales are balanced to perfection and when one visits these places one witnesses unspeakable anguish, hurt, pain, suffering. But make no mistake, this is not the work of a vengeful deity. It is the divine operation of law, balanced to perfection, and those who are in the midst of suffering are there because they have placed themselves there. They can set themselves free when they raise their hearts and minds towards the light and ask for help. But the price has to be paid.

At the opposite end of the spectrum, the other extreme, one ventures into the realms of light. Here also, one is still moving within the spheres of desire. I spoke to you of the Summerland. That is a place which is very akin to your world. It is so because many souls who pass into it expect to be where they are. They are familiar with the landscape of your earth with it's architecture, with it's buildings, with it's streets and it's cities, it's trees and it's valleys and streams, oceans. That is what is in their mind. They have a picture, an image, strongly imbedded within them. And they have certain aspects of desire. One who has perhaps worshipped within the Christian faith, or the Buddhist or the Hindu or the Jew, one finds that these traits are deeply embedded and one expects to meet one's saviour!

If you expect to find a train, it is there waiting for you. If you expect to have a car or a boat, it is there for you, because that is what the mind creates. But when one continues to evolve and move beyond the realms of desire one is sloughing off these aspects of the mind and moving more into the realms of pure spirit. Because remember that spirit and mind are not the same. Spirit is the divine creative essence of which you are a part. Mind is an aspect through which it operates. Mind and spirit are closely linked, but then you have desire, the emotional level and that dictates to a degree the operation of spirit and mind through it. As one evolves one moves beyond emotion into the mental states and beyond that into the spiritual states, into the spiritual realms.

Now, for me to speak to you of a life in the higher aspects that does not incorporate a physical body, a physical form, would perhaps be difficult for you to comprehend. But you see it is all a matter of what the mind creates, what it desires. There reaches a point where one realises that the need for a physical body is unnecessary. One does not need limbs. One becomes pure energy, pure light. One is becoming pure and refined. That does not mean that those in the higher realms move about in a gaseous state, in a nebulous form, without any real form or solidity or anything that is characterised in the form of beauty. Far from it! For the ethereal realms at their highest and most wondrous are expressive of such beauty, such an expanse of light and shade, colour and texture, that it is beyond words. But one does not need a physical form in order to appreciate that.

The great teachers in my world are light. Indeed, such are you at this moment, of light. But you are light expressing itself through a limited form. When that limited form falls away then what remains is the pure essence of being and that, my friends, is your pathway, that is your goal.

It is very difficult for me to put into words the higher echelons of spirit because you have no yardstick by which it can be measured. It is like trying to explain a great building or a tree to a microbe, such is the chasm, such is the vastness that exists between one and the other. You see the problem that I face? But perhaps I have been able to explain to you in some way through your clumsy language part of the pristine beauty of the unfoldment of the spirit.

I know nothing of finality. I know nothing of totality. I know nothing of perfection, only that it is that which is to be sought. But as to reaching perfection I know of no one who has done that. I know of no one who has reached the highest and if they have then they have not returned to speak of it. Perhaps because it is an impossibility for such a high and fine vibration to express itself through a lower mind. But when I hear it said that there are seven levels or fourteen levels, when I hear it spoken that there is a fixed creativity, a fixed creation in spirit, then my mind rebels because this is foreign to that which I have encountered. The whole purpose and process of life is one of endless evolution and one finds that as one evolves to higher levels of being one comes into a freedom. A freedom, a true freedom where one can experience, unfettered, unhindered.

You have wonderful lessons taught to you, you know, in your world, by those who use their imaginations and create for you through the means of your television sets programmes that show man reaching out into the universe. But you know, with the unfolding spirit, you can go anywhere. The spirit aspect is everywhere. Where there is a physical universe there is a spiritual universe. There is but one spirit world although it has many expressions, but one can travel to stars, to planets, to worlds that man has no comprehension of, if one desires it. And one can meet with minds that have experiences that are far different to anything of the earthly expression and all of this provides a knowledge and a richness and a teaching and a learning, wisdom that is so profound, so deep that it cannot possibly find a lodgement of expression within man's mind at this level. I struggle for words and yet I have glimpsed this and I know that it is so.

Man's pathway is not set in stone. It is not rigid, it is flexible. It is in accordance with his will and his free will. But his ultimate destiny is one of supreme light because, remember this my friends; you are part of the Great White Spirit. You are part of that supreme entity, that supreme deity, the father of all creation, the mother of all creation. The divine love and light and radiance of everything that is. You are a part of that. I hope that this has been of some little value to you."

Having acknowledged their grateful thanks, members of the gathering then proceeded once more to question the spirit visitor, something which he actively encourages whenever he communicates:

Q: "When somebody from a higher level......a spirit from a higher level descends......in a book that I've read it is possible for that spirit to remain undetected by those of the lower level, is this correct? If they do not wish to be detected they can enter a lower level?"

White Feather: "Are you speaking of a lower level in my world?"

Sitter: "Yes....in your world."

White Feather: "Yes it is possible, it is possible. Although it is not always desirable, it is possible. You must understand that when one goes to these levels one sometimes does so to learn and to observe, in which case one may not wish to be detected. On the other hand, where one goes to work, to provide guidance and try to uplift these souls then it is often desirable to be recognised. But they would see us as light, as beings of light."

Q: "When you said about realms created by what is in the minds of men, what happens to people who get depressed. They feel that they shouldn't be depressed but they are. Is that created in their mind or is that an emotion from somewhere else?"

White Feather: "There are many reasons for depression. You must understand that it is not, in the truest sense of the word the mind that is depressed, it is the operation of the mind through the brain. You see, just as one may be inflicted with a mental illness, it is not the mind that is ill but there is a malfunction in the operation of the mental faculties because there is an imbalance or a disease in the brain. You know sometimes, depression can be caused by a chemical imbalance. Indeed, sometimes the depression itself can cause the chemical imbalance. It is almost a circle in operation. But that does not mean that the individual, the mind, is in any way hurt or imbalanced, merely its operation through the physical organism, the body and the brain. The brain is not the mind. Do you understand that?

You have to make the distinction. You see, sometimes one questions, and I have been asked the question 'What of one who is mentally ill? What of one who is, to use your earthly language 'schizophrenic'? What happens to that individual when they pass into my world?' And again you must apply the teaching which I have just given to you. It is the operation through the brain. It is an imbalance or an imperfection or a fault if you wish to call it that, in the physical make up, that prevents the mind and the spirit from expressing itself in a natural and normal way. When death occurs then the individual does not express these schizophrenic or psychopathic tendencies that it did upon the earth. There is compensation and retribution for this and indeed that soul may have actually chosen to come into that expression, as difficult as that may be for you to comprehend, in order to undergo that experience and extract from it some knowledge and teaching. So I hope that answers your question?"

Sitter: "Yes, thank you."

White Feather: "Good. Then you are wiser than when you came here. That is something that I have achieved and I am proud of that! It's always good to achieve something."

Q: "Obviously you are saying that we shouldn't have too many set ideas about where we are going....we shouldn't put thought forms up, we should allow ourselves to just go....."

White Feather: "It is good to keep an open mind. It is good that the mind is malleable and pliable. However, you should recognise, and you have heard me say this before; that truth is truth is truth. There are certain things that are true and factual and it is good to recognise those, to imbibe those, to live by those for they are the true landmarks, they are the true flagstones upon which the foundations of further knowledge and truth are built. But above and beyond that, keep your minds fluid. Keep your options open. When you adhere to things simply because you have read them or others have spoken them then the mind becomes rigid. It stagnates. Your thoughts become heavy and further and higher truth has difficulty to find a lodgement. It is like the seed trying to find a place to go and it comes up against granite. Then it cannot settle. It has to search for a crevice or a crack. But where the soil is soft and inviting then it easily sinks deeply within it and finds a place to grow. That is what I am speaking of.

The time has come for me to withdraw. I thank you as I always do for your time, for your patience, for your ears, for your minds, for your hearts and for your spirits. May the blessings of the Great White Spirit be ever upon you."

Chapter Six

Overcoming Fear

"Greetings to you all. I am once again pleased to be able to walk within the garden of your thoughts for even though there is much yet to be cultivated, there is a great deal that I see which pleases me. For many of the seeds of truth which have been sown have begun to germinate and to grow and there is much to be admired.

I thought it would be helpful tonight, to speak to you upon a theme which I have addressed before in the past but which I find of some relevance at the moment of speaking to you. It concerns an aspect of yourselves which each of you has yet to address, perhaps like a weed in a garden, and it is this of fear."

With this introduction, White Feather began his address one evening on the subject of fear, something which he had indeed touched upon many times in the past. For in this current climate it seems that the lives of many individuals are blighted in this way and the guide, aware of this fact, seemed determined to emphasise that in truth, we really have nothing to fear:

"Fear you know, is the great enemy of the soul. Fear is the great enemy of the spirit. There are many, many battles being fought upon your world; disease, pestilence, anger, oppression, hatred, greed, selfishness.....but at the root of many of these lies fear. Fear saps and drains away the very vital energies of the spirit. Fear is like a cancer that emerges within the individual and grows, almost and often to the point where it consumes all rational thinking and you know, fear is at the root, at the heart of so much disease and illness upon your earth. And yet you might say to me, 'if fear is upon the earth, what is its purpose? Why does it exist? Does not everything have a purpose? Is not that which is created by the spirit, of the spirit, have a purpose?'

What is the purpose then, of fear? You know, originally and still today, fear is a necessary aspect in some areas of existence. Fear is established and felt and is registered upon all levels of life, even within the humble insect. Within the spider and the fly, within the bird and the fish, you will find fear because fear is necessary at that level to establish the pattern of evolution. Life has evolved because one species has been able to exist, sometimes at the expense of another, to enable the species to survive, to proliferate, to enable the spirit to be made manifest through it. That does not mean to say that the order of life is based upon the foundation of fear, far from it. But fear is an aspect of what you would term the law of the jungle. For it is necessary at that level that form should evolve in order to survive.

But where there is knowledge, where there is a reasoning mind, where there is an ability to think, to analyse, to dissect, to reason, to understand, there comes a dawning that fear is something to be conquered. Fear is something to be mastered. And yet, how do you conquer fear? How do you rid yourself of fear?

You know, the greatest fear is fear of the unknown. Fear of that which is to be. Fear is born largely out of ignorance. Where there is knowledge, where there is understanding, there, fear cannot find a true lodgement within the heart. Learn to put fear aside. Learn to imbibe the qualities of love, tolerance, compassion, understanding, trust and faith. Allied with fact and knowledge.

Knowledge removes fear. Where there is understanding, where there is a realisation, there can be no fear. These are qualities which are of the higher self, which are of the higher spirit being. And we understand that it is difficult at times for you to imbibe these upon your level of matter, when you are in the midst of turmoil, conflict, confusion. Where you have to obtain the coin of your world, where you have to live and breathe and move and have your being. But when you are able to enter into the still pool of calm thought and reflect upon the higher principles of your being, there you will find the light of truth. There you will find the still small voice that whispers to you. The voice that is louder than anything else. Align yourself to the light. Align yourself to the higher principles of your being and you will find that fear will dissolve and evaporate.

Fear is the prime cause of illness in your world. Fear creates blockages, prevents harmony, disturbs the system. It creates a conflict between the higher state of spirit, the mental state, the emotional state and the physical body. Where there is health and wholeness, these levels exist in a wondrous harmony, each vibration harmonising easily and effortlessly with the other. Where there is fear, there is disharmony, there is disruption and one or more of these fields of being is out of sync with the other. What is needed is a synthesis of these levels, a harmony, a bringing together. And this is done through knowledge, through understanding and by harmonising with the self and with the laws that operate within and through the self and of which you are a part.

It does not require complex procedures. It does not require ceremonies or rituals. It requires only that you still the heart and mind. That you still the chatter. Listen to yourself. Listen to your body, what it is telling you. Listen to the feelings that you feel, the energies that circulate and move and have their being within the field of being. Listen to your heart. Listen to your mind. Listen to your emotions, for these things speak to you.

You know, many in your world are ignorant. They live in the realm of the intellect. They do not listen to what their own being is telling them. This you must strive to do. You must strive to sensitise yourself, to sharpen your instincts, to hone them. To listen to the voice of the inner man, the inner self, the higher self. You may refer to this as intuition - it does not matter what label you put upon it - but listen to it.

When you put fear aside, you are beginning to resonate within your true state. You are beginning to vibrate at the true level of your being. You are beginning to open up to the true potential of the higher self, that it may manifest through every part, through every facet of your being. Where you have this energy and vibration, disease cannot gain a foothold. Where there is true harmony there can be no fear, no disease, because you are aligning yourself with yourself. You are aligning yourself with the spirit of which you are an innate part.

I know that I have spoken to you of fear in the past but this is the opportunity for many of you to learn a great lesson. If you look at the great evolved souls in my world you will see that they have passed through fear. Yes, they have experienced fear, they have known fear but they have passed through it. They have moved beyond it. They have mastered it. These great beings of light, whom some would call angels, are those who have achieved this purity and harmony of self. Look at the index of these souls and you will see fear registered there, but they have moved beyond it. There is no fear, because they know that it is of ignorance.

So think upon this, because fear is the enemy of the modern age. Your world is riddled with fear. Everywhere you look there is fear. Fear of tomorrow, fear of yesterday, fear of death, fear of illness, fear of lack of worth, fear of what others say. Fear of what might have been, fear of life. Put these aside. Allow yourself to bathe in the glorious light of the spirit for this is the greatest power in existence. The greatest power, and it is all that you need."

Q: "When you talk about fear, what is the answer to the fear that gets there before you do? You don't want to be frightened but your mind or some part of you has got there first?"

White Feather: "You know, there are some fears which are born out of conditioning and there are some fears which have been learned, perhaps from an early stage in your life or even those which are born out of past experiences and even those from what some would term 'past lives'. And you know, these are fears which are like rivers that run very deep within your being. But always I would say to you that where there is knowledge, where there is a true understanding, then you will find that fear cannot exist."

Discussing the problem on a separate occasion, White Feather equated the difficulty that some souls have in 'letting go' of certain aspects of their lives, often as a result of being fearful of the consequences. He explains that the way of non-attachment is essential to spiritual evolution and the overcoming of fear related conditions:

"You will perhaps, upon reflecting on the events which have transpired in recent times, understand why I urge you to let go of fear. For each of you has, and continues to be confronted by your own fears. If I can use a term from your world; you are living in the 'school of hard knocks', and it is important that you learn above all else to release that which holds you fast to this planet and this sphere of life.

Letting go of that which you hold dear, letting go of that which you fear, these are difficult things to do but they are vitally necessary if you are to unfold the divinity within and break free of this chain of birth and death, of which you are currently a part.

Those of you who are familiar with the Buddhist teachings will perhaps be aware of that knowledge which speaks of the way of non-adherence, the way of non-attachment, and here is a great lesson for you all. For if you are attached to anything which is external to you, whether it be a person, a place, an object, an idea, a creed, a teaching.....whatever, and you come to rely upon that source for your happiness and contentment, then I say to you that you will not progress unless you can learn to let it go.

It is difficult I know, because naturally through the course of events you become attached and familiar with the patterns of life which are formed early on in your physical span. These pathways become well entrenched and habitual, so that you think in a certain way and you are conditioned to react in a certain way to a given stimulus. But the way of the masters is the way of non-attachment.

True happiness lies within yourself. True contentment, true peace, true understanding, lies within yourself, and you must be critical with yourself, honest and perceptive in your judgement of yourself and your interactions and relationship with all that is around you. And if you can do this and emerge purified from it without having to rely upon it, then you are truly upon the pathway of spiritual unfoldment."

Occasionally the spirit guide will tell a story which relates to his own time upon earth, usually to help illustrate a particular point. This juncture seemed an opportune moment to do just that:

" I remember all too well an incident which occurred in my youth, and you know how I like to tell you stories! We did not fish with rods. We were not quite as sophisticated as that, but we did enjoy standing in the great flowing waters of the river and immersing our hands in the water to wait for the fish that we knew would inevitably come along. The idea, the teaching, was to gently cup the hands around the fish and scoop it out of the water and throw it onto the bank. But of course when the great fish comes along there is often the desire to hold onto it and to show everyone and to shout out 'look what I have caught!'. This I did, but to my horror, the fish proved to be a little stronger than I and it took me down into the water because my pride would not let go.

When you go to your bank manager to ask for a loan, he says; 'Yes, you can borrow the money but you must pay it back'. Everything has its price. The price of pride is often a fall. That which you cling to, clings to you. That to which you hold fast, holds on to you. The teaching which I am giving you is from the heart. It is not a teaching which says you must be selfish, that you must put self first, that you must not love others, that you must not care for them, that you must not forge relationships with others and with that which you love. But part of letting go of fear is letting go also of that to which you hold fast."

It seems that being honest with ourselves is an important part of learning to deal with our fears. The spirit sage underlined this aspect when addressing a small gathering one evening. His words, as so often spoken, seemed to relate to a far wider audience than those present:

" You knew before you came upon this pathway the work to be undertaken. The journey to this point in time has been long, has been difficult, has been fraught with setbacks, hardships, all of which have been necessary to sharpen your senses. To strengthen you, to revitalise you and to hone your spiritual insight and inner sense for the tasks ahead.

However, the first lesson that you must each learn, and I include the one through whom I speak to you, is to eradicate fear. Because each of you holds fear within you. It is not a fear of linking with us. When you sit you are not in fear, but each of you holds fear. Whether it be fear of failure, fear of disappointment, fear of rejection, fear of pain, fear of illness.....and it is necessary for you to undergo a critical self examination, to look at yourselves, your vices and virtues. This cannot be done by any external agency, but by you as an individual.

Realise that you carry within you both the negative and positive aspects and energies that comprise the duality of being. Within you are the male and female energies, the dark and the light, the positive and the negative. In order for the work to be undertaken, there must be a balancing, a harmony and a recognition of these energies as they work through you. An understanding of the law of opposites and the law of attraction. To do this you must begin to recognise your faults and your imperfections, not in a way that distresses you or causes you heartache, but in a purposeful way, in a positive manner, to learn to eradicate fear that saps and drains the very vital forces of life, which prevents harmony and peace from reigning supreme in your life. To do this you must be scrupulously honest with yourselves. But this is the way of the masters. This is the way of spiritual verity and spiritual growth. Fear and ignorance are the hub which is at the centre of the wheel of birth and death. This continuous cycle which encompasses Karmic law and which decrees that an individual shall return time and time again to this world to put right the imbalance of past lives. But you should bear witness to my words and look within yourselves and go deeply into the heart of your being. REMOVE ALL FEAR. Realise that fear is the enemy of the spirit. Realise that you have within you such love, such light, such radiant beauty, such richness, such strength."

It is encouraging to know that despite our fears and imperfections, we each have within us the means to eradicate our weaknesses. To overcome those things which disturb the balance of our minds and often lead to physical illness. From what the spirit world tell us we can perhaps begin to recognise that we truly are the architects of our own destiny, and the very pathway along which each of us walks is in accordance with our own thoughts and actions. It naturally follows then, that to change our thinking ultimately changes our future.

Chapter Seven

Influencing the Body of Matter

White Feather has often spoken of how our thoughts and actions have an effect upon the various levels of our being, but what is little understood is the way in which our present day attitudes and lifestyles also have a bearing upon future incarnations of souls about to be born into this world, particularly in terms of the actual genetics involved. In this talk the guide tackles this complex subject and explains how, both individually and collectively, we have a great responsibility towards future generations:

" Greetings. It is good that once more we have this opportunity for dialogue with you. For it is on these occasions that we are able to impart that truth that we seek to give in order to bring about a greater realisation and awareness of what truly is.

We are often asked the question of whether the behaviour of humanity has any effect upon the outworking of the spiritual plan that seeks ever to unfold and to reveal its innermost beauty. Whilst it is true that man can hinder, man can delay the outworking of the plan, ultimately he will not prevent its fulfilment. For as I have said on many occasions; spirit is master, matter is servant, and the will of the divine spirit must outwork itself.

However, it has to be stated that man, through his actions can influence the degree in which the spirit can express itself upon your world. For what affects the body of matter also has its effect upon the spirit, in the way that the spirit can manifest upon your earth. Just as equally, what affects the spirit can have its effect upon the body of matter. What is of concern is the disturbing trend that seems to be evolving in your world, that is leading to an indiscipline, a disregard for authority, a disregard for the adherence to the laws of the land. A lack of respect for those in positions of responsibility. It seems that this attitude is being bred into successive generations in your world and it affects not only individuals, but also entire sections of society, and this is having an effect on the way in which successive incarnations into your world of matter can affect their link with that body of matter.

Try to understand that when a soul incarnates into the body of matter of your world at the moment of conception, there are two main aspects at work. One, is the individual spirit that is about to incarnate, that brings with it the knowledge, wisdom, awareness, understanding that it has gained from previous lives and experiences, and also the material and etheric aspects with which it has to link, to blend and to harmonise; to create the new body of matter through which it can manifest upon your earth. This latter aspect presents a challenge to the incoming spirit in that it has to equate its linking with your world with the substance and material that it is given to work with. The etheric, the genetic material that is created largely through the DNA coding that is passed through the genes of the parents. And it has to be said that frequently, the material that is presented to the incarnating spirit is not that which it should be.

Perhaps I can draw simile with life upon your world many centuries ago, when the caveman walked upon the earth with a form that was far less refined than modern man. A form whose physical development was still in its early stages of unfoldment. The degree of spirit expression through this form was very limited. The intellectual, reasoning, emotional, mature thinking individual that is now so often found in your world could not have expressed itself in that epoch in time. For there was not the physical machinery, the earthly vehicle, to facilitate it.

It is perhaps like asking a great musician to play a symphony upon a tin whistle. It would be an impossibility to do so, to any great degree of worth. And yet, as the body becomes refined, so more and more of the spirit, a greater expression of the spirit can become apparent. The finer the substance the quicker in vibration the etheric material, and the greater the genetic programming, the more finely constructed can the physical body become and this in turn facilitates a greater expression of the spirit mind that comes into it.

The difficulties arise when through incorrect thinking and actions, the genetic code of the DNA within the collective unconscious of humanity becomes altered and successive generations have to encounter the consequences of that alteration, and even though the spirit can often compensate and overcome minor fluctuations, where there has been a persistent change of the mental, emotional and physical state then this can produce lasting changes at this level of being and the material that is presented to the incoming spirit is somewhat lower in its vibration, cruder in its composition."

It seemed as though the spirit guide was inferring here that the actions of humanity, stretching back over recent history, had resulted in changes occurring at a genetic level which have in turn had an effect upon the way in which incarnating souls can link with this world. For despite the fact that there are still many spiritually aware people upon the earth it is also evident that there are many hundreds of thousands of individuals who live their lives in complete ignorance of moral and spiritual laws and truths. Indeed, the decline in the level of morality has been so marked as to have been noticeable within the lifetime of many reading these words. The guide went on to explain further the implications involved:

"You may ask the question why it seems that as you look around you there are so many minds, particularly amongst the young of your world, who have this attitude of mind and body. This rebellious nature, where it seems they cannot be controlled, where they have no respect for their parents, for those around them. Where there is, seemingly, this self destructive nature which I often refer to as 'the culture of want', where the 'I' is more important than anything. Where the ego rises to become prevalent over the higher aspects of the spirit that seek expression.

It seems to be self perpetuating, for it has to be stated that what is sowed is reaped. If ignorance is sown, then ignorance will be reaped. If darkness is sown, then darkness will be reaped and it is this against which we have a constant struggle.

This is why so many minds at this moment in time are drawing close to your world and incarnating into your world of matter, to try and raise the vibrations. To lift man's understanding to a higher plateau of awareness, that this, in turn, can feed back into his genetic and etheric make up, to bring about a quickening and a refinement that will facilitate, in successive generations, a higher aspect of spirit being able to manifest upon your world.

It is a complex issue and one which many in your world will have difficulty in comprehending. You must understand that every thought, every word, every deed, every action, every emotion, every desire has its effect upon your body of matter and upon the body of spirit.

Your etheric and spiritual bodies are not fixed. Just as your physical body is not fixed, it changes from moment to moment. Just as the cells in your physical body are born and then die, to be replaced by others, so there is a constant fluctuation within the energies of your higher bodies as they respond to the various thoughts, emotions, aspirations that pass through your mind and your whole being.

If the music which you play upon your instrument is of a fine quality then it affects the quality of your bodies, on all levels. If the music of your soul can express itself then you will find that your whole being quickens. If, on the other hand you align yourself to the lower aspects of life you will find that your vibrations lower correspondingly and over a period of time this can become more pronounced."

Speaking further about what he termed 'the collective unconscious of humanity' the spirit teacher went on to explain how each of us as individuals, carry a responsibility to ensure that we strive always to reach out to the very highest that we can in all aspects of our lives:

" You see, the actions of each of you as individuals also contribute to what I call 'the collective unconscious of humanity' and that collective unconscious can be of a higher nature or of a somewhat lower nature in its composition. Thus, when you have a soul who is about to incarnate into your world of matter, it has to contend with that which is presented to it from this collective unconscious and from its parents, in order to shape, create and manifest through the body of matter. It follows then, does it not, that where individuals can live lives of higher aspiration, of service, of giving, imbibing the qualities of love, tolerance, compassion, understanding, illumination, it affects not only their individual bodies, which are quickened, but ultimately it has its effect upon the collective unconscious of humanity, raising its vibration to a higher plateau of being and thus facilitating a quicker vibration for those generations of souls who are to follow you by incarnating into the body of matter.

You have a greater responsibility the greater awareness that you have. The greater the awareness, the more responsibility that you have to yourself and those around you, to all of humanity. Align yourself to the light. Align yourself to the power, to the wisdom, to the truth of the spirit. Allow these things to express themselves in your life. In doing so you will be doing a service not only to yourself and the Great Spirit, but to your children and your children's children. For everything that you do, every aspect of your life is registered indelibly at some level. Nothing is ever lost. Nothing is ever wasted or forgotten.

The greater that man can aspire, the greater that man can raise his vibrations, the more that the spirit can express itself and the greater that expression the more beauty and richness can be made available in the world of matter. This is, we know, a complex teaching but we ask you as always to think upon it. Disregard that with which you cannot find allegiance. Harmonise with that which you find comes within the orbit of your own understanding. We thank you."

Despite White Feather's teaching on how our thoughts and actions influence our genetic programming and that, what mankind sows, he reaps, there are those who still believe that there is genuine evil at play in the universe and that perhaps this even emanates from what they term 'The Devil'. This is what the learned helper had to say on this aspect of ignorance:

"It must be stated quite categorically that whilst there is undoubtedly an element of goodness and evil at work in your world, evil as an entity, personified through what your orthodox teachers call 'the Devil,' is non-existent. Everything has its opposite. To joy there is sorrow, to freedom there is captivity, to darkness there light, to knowledge and truth there is ignorance, to hope there is doubt and to goodness there is evil. But these things are not intrinsic within the psyche of man. They are elements and aspects of the one, which are embraced in degree, in accordance with the mind and the purpose and the will of the individual.

Perhaps I can draw for you the analogy of a river. All rivers have their source. That source, that spring from which that river, however mighty, however broad, however long it may be, emerges, is very often pure. As it begins its descent to the ocean, it may wander and as it deepens and broadens it may become polluted and tainted by elements and aspects which it absorbs into itself to such a degree that it may become VERY tainted, VERY dark, laden with pollutants. But it is always a river, it always contains within it the potential for purity, for cleansing. And so it is with every spark of the divine which commences upon this pathway of unfoldment."

The guide went on to outline the danger of allowing that aspect of the mind known as the 'ego' to become inflated and how this could lead to all manner of problems, both for the individual and for society in general:

" What must be understood is that as one experiences through life, one has certain desires and needs which have to be fulfilled and met. Very often the ego self is fed and nurtured out of all proportion and this dictates, through the personality, the desires of the individual. The soul, which is the guiding principle, which is the divine essence, is often denied its expression. I have spoken to you before, where I have said to you of the conscience. The conscience which speaks to you, so that every individual, regardless of their state of progress has a guiding principle, a compass point if you like within themselves, which orders this balance of right and wrong so that they know innately, right from wrong, good from bad. But where the personality dictates and where the needs of the ego predominate, there, this of the soul principle is often denied and the ability to measure, to judge, to weigh up and to recognise right from wrong is often distorted."

The spirit visitor then outlined a truth which he suggested would make all of those present think very deeply:

" Very often you know, and this will make you think......and I want you to think very deeply on this; that which you look upon and you despise as being selfish or hateful, this of jealousy, this of greed......is the need for the soul to love itself, to express itself. But its expression becomes distorted through the personality body, through the ego body, and its essence becomes lost. But if you really think about this and upon this, you will realise that much which is of darkness is but a striving for light to express itself.
Now that may sound a contradiction to you. It may be difficult for you to grasp, to understand, but if you think upon it you will find that it is true."

Bringing his talk to its conclusion, White Feather underlined the truth that every soul has the opportunity for redemption and reaffirmed that evil exists only within the minds of men:

" However low the soul may descend, to whatever depths of depravity and darkness, the divine within it can never be extinguished. The very lowest of low is bound with the highest of high. Within every murderer, within every despot, within every cheat and liar and drunkard is a part of you. You are not separate from them. You cannot divorce yourself from them because you are part of them. The spirit does not discriminate. The spirit is not held within one and not within another. The thread of the spirit, of the divine, runs throughout the weave of life, creating its pattern within the fabric of substance in all its wondrous and diverse expression. Throughout the microcosm and the macrocosm, within complexity and simplicity there is spirit in degree.

When you look at your brother and you see within him evil, it is not evil born from a deity. It is evil created by misrepresentation and misguidance and misunderstanding. It is not beyond redemption. That individual is not beyond change, beyond saving. It is all a matter of allowing the spirit within to express itself in its fullness, in its radiance, in its beauty. You have much work to do, not only upon your world but in mine also.

Let me say this to you; you may wonder why it is that there is a preponderance, an escalation of what you call evil in your world. Why there is more anger and war and bloodshed. Let me say that violence perpetuates violence, darkness gives rise to darkness, hatred breeds hatred. It is the coin of life. Thought forms play a major part in what is occurring upon your world. For there is a preponderance of selfish thought forms, of evil thoughtforms, of dark thought forms. There is an escalation of those who tamper with substances, taking those substances into their physical form and their etheric body also. There is an escalation in many areas of this and all of this creates thought forms and draws energies around the individual, throughout your world. Those in my world, who have passed through this and who have taken their lives either knowingly or unknowingly through this, are drawn to these thought forms and to these individuals. Just as we are drawn to you out of your spiritual light, so they are drawn by darkness. So you see, it is a chain reaction. It is self regenerating and it is this which must be addressed. It is this which must be checked. You have a great amount of work to do.

Let me say that you are used also in the sleep state. This is why sometimes you are a little weary when you awaken because you are used, not in the sense that you are compelled......it is because you have chosen.....but your vehicle of the spirit is used and your mind is used to help those in the astral planes of life.

But remember that evil, like goodness, is the opposite side of the coin. There is no one who is intrinsically evil. All have the divine seeds bestowed within them. The seeds of perfection. And all will be gathered in and will stand radiant in the light of spiritual knowledge and truth."

Chapter Eight

Karma

Karmic law is something upon which White Feather has spoken on numerous occasions, as indeed have many other learned minds, and yet this aspect of spiritual teaching still seems to be misunderstood. With the current interest in 'past life regression' and other such phenomena it may well be of interest to the reader to hear the guide's views on this fascinating subject:

" Today we will bring you a teaching that concerns what is termed 'Karmic Law'. But to begin, we must firstly clarify what is meant by the law of Karma. For there are many in your world who believe, mistakenly, that the law of cause and effect is in fact the law of Karma. Now whilst it is true that cause and effect play their part within the operation of Karmic law, it must be clearly understood that Karma holds much more significance than the mere operation of the law of cause and effect. For Karmic law is linked directly with the unfolding consciousness of individuals and the personal responsibility that, that awakening brings. For the more aware one becomes, the greater responsibility one has for one's thoughts, words and deeds, and it is one thing to undertake an action in ignorance and quite another to do so in knowledge and understanding. And it has to be recognised, the greater one moves up the scale of spiritual unfoldment, the greater the responsibility, the greater the impact of Karmic law.

But let us first give an example with which you can associate, so as to explain in simple terms the difference. If you put your hand into a flame, perhaps by chance, and that flame then burns your skin and causes you pain, then it can be said that here is the operation of cause and effect. The cause being your hand entering the fire and the effect, as a result of that, being the blistering of the skin and the resulting pain. If however, you deliberately put your hand into the fire in order to inflict pain upon yourself or perhaps you put the hand of another into the fire in order to inflict pain upon them, then not only do you evoke the law of cause and effect but also the law of Karma. For what comes into question is the motive, the purpose of your actions.

You see, everything has a price. The price of increased sensitivity is increased responsibility and whilst you cannot exhibit perfection at this level of being, because the lesser cannot express the greater, nevertheless you have unfolded a degree of freewill that is linked to the level of awareness, knowledge and understanding that you have been able to unfold. And thus, your thoughts and your actions must be justified. For the law operates as I have said on many occasions, with a wonderful precision and where an individual or a group of individuals has undertaken a particular course of action with knowledge, knowing that course of action will result in a specific outcome, then always the law reflects a measured response. And if that act results in pain and suffering to others, to life.....whether it be human, animal, bird, insect, fish.....then the price has to be paid. Always the scales have to be balanced and injustice has to be righted."

Stressing that neither God nor anyone else pronounces judgement over us, the teacher went on to explain that in order for us to progress, we have to work out our debts and put right that which we have done wrong:

" It is not a question of judgement by the Great Spirit. It is not a question of revenge. But it is a question of balance and the law of Karma determines precisely how and when that balance is reached. Sometimes I am asked the question, 'What of the lesser brethren of your world, how does the law of

Karma affect them? Perhaps when one creature destroys another or when one species of plant encroaches upon another?' But here again, you must recognise that there is not the same level of awareness, of understanding, of conscious expression and thus there is not the same degree of responsibility. When the blackbird eats the worm it does not do so out of any motive other than to feed its hunger. When the lion attacks the zebra it does so only that its appetite can be fed. And yet man, so often destroys other physical life, not merely to satisfy his own appetite, but out of desire for revenge or through anger, or jealousy, or hatred, or malice of some kind. This is where the higher law of Karma comes into play."

The spirit guide continued his talk by placing emphasis on the outworking of Karmic law, however long that might take, stressing that many of our current life problems may be attributable to what we ourselves had sown by our past actions:

" You must understand also, that the law fulfills itself in varying degrees of time. And even though you may have forgotten an action which you undertook many years or even lifetimes ago, the law does not forget and that which has been sown, has to be reaped.

There are times of course when the Karma that is reaped is instant, such as when you put your hand into the fire, but many times it appears that justice is not done in your world or in your physical lifetime, where an individual undertakes an action that goes unpunished. But I say to you, always the law operates to perfection and that which is sown is reaped.

Have you ever questioned why it is that one is born into your world, perhaps carrying the burden of a particular physical deformity or mental aberration? Perhaps where one is born into poverty or disease or famine? It has to be recognised that very often, this is the result of Karmic law and the soul has chosen for that facet which is undertaking that particular incarnation, the conditions which it knows will facilitate the greatest lessons being learned to enable service to be rendered and the balance to be redressed. For only when the scales are level and what has to be accrued in a past life has been evened out, and healed, and neutralised, can the soul move on to higher things and greater experiences.

Remember that you are never alone in this quest for unfoldment. Many who undertake to repay a Karmic debt do so with those around them who have chosen to help at this time. Frequently, when you are reintroduced into the body of matter you will find that those with whom you link intimately, you have known before. They have chosen to help you, as indeed you may have chosen to help and assist them in this particular phase of life.

Karmic law may take but a few moments to outwork itself, or it may take many aeons of time. But only when it has outworked itself, will the soul progress as it should do."

Although the guide had previously intimated that increased awareness and responsibility could lead to a greater Karmic debt being accrued should one knowingly commit a wrong, he explains here how progress also leads to a greater awareness of error and that the higher one climbs, in spiritual terms, the less likely it becomes that mistakes will be made:

" Try to understand that the more that you do progress, in a sense the less of an impact Karmic law has upon you because you are less likely to err in the way that you have done previously and so there is less to outwork, less to balance, less to correct. The pathway, in a sense, becomes easier and smoother.

When you move out of ignorance and into understanding, when you emerge from darkness to light, then your awareness brings to you a wisdom that enables you to think and to act in a more controlled and disciplined, responsible way. And this of course, quickens your soul. It speeds your evolution into the realms of light.

Never fear Karma. Never fear the Great Spirit or the operation of the law.

Whatever you have undertaken, whether it is in ignorance or in knowledge, remember that there will be the opportunity to correct it. Even in this life in which you now live upon the earth, if you are aware that your actions may have incurred a Karmic debt, do not despair, but begin to correct that which you have done. If you have hurt or injured another, then even though it may not be possible to receive their forgiveness at this moment, seek to redress the balance by helping others. By giving of yourself in service, freely and unfettered, imbibing the qualities of love, compassion, tolerance, understanding. Allowing the higher aspects of your soul and of the Great Spirit to manifest through you.

For service is the key. Service is a way in which you can repay your debt. It is one way of helping you to reclaim lost ground. Put back that which you have taken out. Correct that which have disturbed through your actions.

There are many who, in your world, incur so much Karmic debt that it will take great efforts on their behalf, perhaps over many lifetimes, to repay and put right that which has been wronged. But even individuals such as this still come within the light of the Great Spirit, for no one is forgotten or neglected or swept aside. No one is condemned to hell or eternal damnation. For all are parts of the Great Spirit and even though you, through your endeavours, through your free will, actions and deeds, may be like seeds scattered to the farthest corners of the earth, all will be gathered in, in the harvest of the Great Spirit. All who have gone forth will be reclaimed. all will be counted back. You are the children of the great universal intelligence from which you emerged and are ever a part.

So think upon this teaching and you will find that when you are aware, perhaps more acutely aware of your actions and thoughts, you will guard them a little more carefully. You will choose your words and you will watch your actions, not in fear and trepidation, but in the light of the responsibility which you have. And let me say this in conclusion; that providing your motive is always true, providing it is selfless and seeks always that which is right, then you will not go far wrong. It is only when you allow the lower emotions to dominate your thoughts and your actions, that you find that you go astray. Remember the conscience, which is the compass of the soul within. It always guides you to the truth. Follow it, listen to it, adhere to its tenets and you will find that it will always point you to the light."

At one small gathering of the development group during which White Feather often communicates, the guide gave more insight into the operation of Karmic law and how, when reincarnating, an individual can incorporate aspects of their past existence in a new earthly life. He also touched upon the concept of 'group Karma' which many readers may find interesting:

"You must understand the operation of the law in the way that it applies to each of you, through your Karma as individuals and as a group. It is true that you have been together in what you call 'past lives' beforehand. You have incarnated together because you are part of the same soul group. Therefore, you have incurred not only individual Karma, but group Karma which must be outworked, must complete itself.

Although it is not always the same aspect of your individuality that incarnates into a physical body, nevertheless it is a part of the whole, and that aspect which comes upon this earth as it has done at this time, does so having acquired a level of evolvement and development and also a Karmic debt, which is why you should be aware of your responsibilities now and the pathway which has lead you to this point.

There are certain aspects of your unfoldment which have still to be understood and certain conditions which have yet to be cleared. This we call Karma. This is why the time that you are here now is of the utmost importance. You have this work to do as a group and as individuals. If you do not all play your part, then the consequences will be felt by the whole.

This is what you must understand. We know of the fears that you have in your hearts. You think that some of you are inadequate. You think that you are here to, if I may use your phraseology 'make up the numbers'. That is not so. You are parts, again I repeat, of one whole."

Many believe, that where a particular fear or phobia exists within an individual, it may be as a result of past trauma, possibly from a previous incarnation. White Feather explains how this can in fact, be so:

"When a facet incarnates into the physical body, it must follow that, that physical body has been earned by its previous pathway. Let me give you an example; If a soul departs from this life by drowning, then there is a distinct probability that in the next incarnation there will be a fear of water, or a dislike of depths of water. But you say, 'How can this be if it is a different facet of the individual which incarnates?' Again, you must understand that when that facet of the individuality links with the mental level of being, it cannot exclude itself from what has gone before. This fear may be very deep seated, may be on a subconscious level, the very depths of the mind, and yet it is there. It is only by recognising it, by facing it, by bringing it to the surface, that it can be understood and its Karmic influence can be outworked."

It is clear from these teachings, that we should each strive to take responsibility for our actions at all times and that we alone must face the consequences of what we think, do and say. What is comforting however, is that we are always given help, not only by those in the spirit realms who desire to see us progress, but also by those upon this world whom we recognise as our families and friends.
Who knows how many times we have each lived and linked together before. Perhaps only time will reveal this to us, as we each strive to progress towards the summit of life.

Chapter Nine

Gifts of the Spirit

As we pass through this life we are often privileged to work with and observe people who seem to be endowed with the most wonderful abilities. Great musicians, artists, writers, poets, healers......the list seems endless. But where do these gifts originate? Are they cultivated here upon the earth? Are they a result of our genetic inheritance? Or do we bring them with us when we incarnate? One evening, after entrancing his medium and making his entrance, White Feather proceeded to elaborate upon the subject to the interest of all present:

" Tonight I want to speak to you briefly, because time as always, is at a premium, about gifts. Not the gifts that you wrap in paper and give on special occasions, but the gifts with which each of you are endowed. The gifts of the Great White Spirit. For it seems that in your world in particular, there is a great deal of confusion about that which is a true spiritual gift and that which is either a materially acquired skill or an inherited trait. For the true gifts of the spirit cannot be manufactured, cannot be artificially induced or created by man. They are there because the individual has earned the right to have acquired them and they do not tarnish, rust or decay, but endure into all eternity and can be exhibited in degree from lifetime to lifetime upon the physical plane of being.

Let me give you an example; You have, hypothetically shall we say, a man and a woman, a male and a female, who both have great musical talent. They marry and give birth to an offspring who, at a very early age exhibits great musical awareness and skill and whom you might term a child prodigy. It is naturally assumed that the gifts that the child possesses are the direct result of the blending of its parents, of the genes and chromosomes that are brought together to form this new body. Whilst this is partially true, it must be understood that there is an individual spirit soul that has linked with that particular personality and entered into that incarnation. Which has earned the right to express itself through that form and may bring to it, gifts of a similar nature, which it exhibits at an early age.

Because you see, the form that you acquire is the form which you have earned and which you yourselves choose to express yourselves through in order to exhibit what gifts and talents you have and further develop the faculties of your nature which are as yet imbalanced and undeveloped. And it is, I would say, almost an impossibility for one who has not earned the right and not acquired the gifts to express itself through such a form.

It is a blending of the two states of being - the spiritual and the material. Never is it and never should it be understood or viewed that it is a purely material process."

Speaking to members of the gathering who were recognised healers, the spirit sage used this ability as an example to further illustrate his point:

"To take your example; you have the ability to direct the healing power through yourselves as channels to those who are in need. You realise of course, that YOU do not have the healing power. It is true that you give of your own magnetic energies, but I am talking of the power of the spirit. You are only channels through which it comes.

But a closer examination will reveal two important aspects. Firstly, you are able to be channels because you have the necessary etheric and physical constitution which enables this power to be generated through you. But more importantly, you have earned the right, spiritually, to be able to manifest yourselves through these physical channels and to open yourselves up, by what means you call attunement, to this great benign power. Had you not earned the right to become healers then you would not be healers, because the power could not be put through you to any significant degree.

You see, it is always a combination of the spiritual and the material. There are those who acquire material skills, which can be developed to a very high degree, but the gifts of the spirit are eternally endowed and eternally earned and they can be, and are, transferred when the individual passes into my world at death. They do not decay. They do not tarnish. So the gifts which you have now, may have been acquired initially, many, many lifetimes ago when you were upon the earth. Perhaps many centuries ago. But they are gifts of the soul, gifts of the self. Forget personality, we are talking now of individuality and once you have acquired these gifts, then in different lifetimes they can be brought to the surface and they can exhibit themselves."

Although, because we all originate from the same divine source, we each have the potential for mediumship, White Feather has always stressed that true mediums are born, not manufactured. However, it is still apparent that even spiritual gifts need to be unfolded:

" Sometimes you have gifts in a particular incarnation, which cannot express themselves. But nevertheless they are there, buried deep with your being. This is why, particularly in those of you who are mediumistic, these gifts have to be developed, because they are buried deep within the persona. They have to be brought to the surface.

Many people make the mistake of thinking that you learn to become a medium. You do not learn. It is a case of training what is already there, cultivating what already exists. Just as a gardener cannot create a beautiful rose or a great vine, or a wondrous tree. He can only train it, give it his love and attention and his guidance, and the beauty that is within it will be brought out. You cannot create beauty, you cannot truly create talent, it is there and you can help it and guide it.

So my friends, my message to you tonight is to cultivate your true spiritual gifts. These are many and numerous. Not just the obvious, which are at the surface of your being, but those which lie a little deeper, beyond the surface. The gifts of patience, of tolerance, of understanding, of compassion, of love, of strength, of inner resolution and resolve, of quietness, of stillness. These are the gifts of the spirit and a great soul exhibits these in abundance.

Forget the great platitudes that are given to those who work in your world, simply because they are able to demonstrate some particular psychic gift. The real gifts are the spiritual ones. There are very few in your world who are truly spiritual. You are privileged because you sit together in harmony and you link with the great spiritual light. That light comes from the circle of the White Brotherhood. It is the great light of the spirit and it fills each one of you with its radiance. There is no greater light than this and no greater privilege to sit and bathe within its radiance.

May the blessings of the Great White Spirit enfold you all with their love. May his presence always watch over you. May his heart beat with your heart beat and may you always walk together along this endless pathway. Peace be with you."

At a separate gathering one of the sitters raised the topic of achievement, suggesting that it is only through hard work that anything worthwhile is accomplished:

Q: "It seems to me that if you want to do anything you have to work hard at it and sometimes it's as if you are not getting anywhere at all, and then if you keep working at it, eventually you get some kind of reward from it...."

White Feather: "Well, that is very true. You have answered your own question in a sense. You know, when you work hard at something there comes a point, almost a moment in time, when it suddenly becomes easy because you have crossed that threshold. Perhaps a threshold of skill, a threshold of ability or awareness or growth. Or perhaps a combination of all of these things. But for anything to be easy there has to have been, at some point, a great deal of endeavour. Now, even those born into your world....and this is an interesting point to have touched upon.....there are those born into your world who have many, many gifts. I am speaking of natural gifts. Perhaps a gift of music or art....a Beethoven, a T.S Elliot, a Shakespeare, an Einstein, and you say 'where has this come from?' They bring it with them! Because they have learned, they have gained knowledge and the right to receive further knowledge by their previous endeavours, so that it appears very easy for them. But this belies the hard work that they have undertaken, perhaps in a previous existence."

Speaking of his own experiences in communicating through his medium, the spirit mentor disclosed how difficult it had been at times to put his message across:

"You know, it took me a great deal of time before I was able to communicate through this instrument because there had to be a great deal of work undertaken. A great deal of training, of sensitisation, achieved through pain, through heartache, through despair, before the sensitivity was achieved and I could step into the breach and make myself known. A great many years elapsed before I could do this. I linked with this instrument before, BEFORE he came upon the earth. I have said this to you before, but that was so. We agreed to do this work, but it was very difficult for me, frustrating, to have to stand back in a sense, not being able to give what I wanted to. But I knew that it was necessary.

You have souls who work with you, I might add, who have undergone and continue to undergo the same experiences, and you yourselves may one day be in this position. The roles are reversed and you will feel the frustration that is allied to this. But I trust that you will also have by then, the wisdom, the knowledge, the foresight to see that it is necessary. But everything that is worthwhile achieving has to be through hard work. There are no short cuts.....none."

As so often happens when White Feather begins answering the many questions which are asked of him, the topic in question is broadened by those who, having listened to what has been said, introduce another facet to the debate. Although the following question concerns a personal situation, readers may find the answer given helpful :

Q: "I've got a book at home of writings......what I'd like to know is, why did I get them? Are they true or are they straight out of my mind? And if they are good, why did I stop getting them?

White Feather: "There was a time when, may I say that you had a greater link than you now have with those minds in my world. You are aware of the circumstances which altered that link. That is not a criticism, it does not mean that you have somehow become retarded in your spiritual growth. It merely means that there has been a change. Mediumship ebbs and flows, it is not constant. There is change. You reach a plateau and it is as if you tap a rich vein of knowledge and truth, just as if you open a well-spring and a great river begins to pour forth and after a while that river begins to dry up and dwindles to nothing and you wonder why? Perhaps it is that there is needed a change, a challenge, an alteration in direction for whatever purposes that relate to that individual. What you have received in the past may have been necessary for you at that time. What you receive today in the way that you work, you do so because it is right for you at this time. Who is to say......who am I to say that you will not once again reach a pinnacle, a plateau, and become open for another great river to flow through you?

You see, it is difficult for you in your world to maintain the status quo. You are touching here upon higher levels of thought and spirituality which are not always conducive to the conditions that lie in your world. You have many things to change you. You have fears, you have self consciousness, you have doubts, you wonder whether it is your own thoughts, whether it is something that you have conjured up from your unconscious, and these things prevent harmony. They change the energies that can work through. But if they do so, it does not mean that you have failed, it merely means that there is a change because it is right, there is a change because you are not ready at that moment. So I answer you with great love and kindness because I never seek to hurt or to injure. But it is so that you reached a point, a pinnacle, the top of the mountain and you touched upon it for a little while and now you have moved a little lower into the valley of experience to learn something new, in a different way.

Purity is seldom maintained for any length of time upon the earth. Because the earthly conditions are very impure and many streams run into your stream. This is a fact. It is difficult I know to take on board, difficult to understand, but it is so.

I am aware of what you say. I have not read your words and I do not need to because I look into your heart and that is a better guide for me. I hope that has answered your question."

Different Sitter: "Can I ask something......because sometimes you find yourself doing things......and I don"t know, you get intuition and you think, where did that come from? How do I know that? I've never been taught how to operate in that way! Or sometimes you approach a situation, have a choice to make and the first thing that comes into your mind....you think 'Oh yes"....and then you change your mind and then you go back and wish you had done the first thing.....but alright, you didn't.....so can you just tell us about intuition?"

White Feather: "Is that a question or an essay!? Yes, I humour you with great love! Yes, intuition, where does it come from? Where does it go to? Who is inspired? Who is the inspired one? And who is the inspirer? And is not the inspirer himself inspired? There are many channels, many fountains of wisdom in my world who send forth inspiration and they send it forth because they seek to help others who are climbing the mountain of unfoldment. It is like rolling a pebble down a mountainside. The one who stands at the summit, who throws that pebble and watches it bounce and tumble and roll down the mountainside.....he has no idea where it will land or who will collect it or into whose pocket it may fall. And yet someone down below gathers it, picks it up, admires it, puts it away in his pocket. Or maybe he himself wishes to show it to another and that other wishes then to share it with someone else. And so from a tiny spark, a great roaring flame of fire is created. From that tiny pebble, many minds are touched.

The inspiration which I give to you may inspire you to give to another, but I also am inspired. As I am a guide to this instrument, so I myself am guided. And those who guide me are guided. I have no awareness as I speak to you, of the guide of the guide of the guide who guides me! I am only aware that I speak to you out of my own resources of knowledge but also by other minds with whom I link who are more knowledgeable than I. They themselves link with other minds and so on and so forth.

So you see, it is like a tumbling waterfall. But of course you also have your own intuition. Your own guidance from your own higher mind, from your soul. Now, not all have earned the right to register that in your world. Some register it but do not know they register it. Some have inspiration and intuition but do not know from whence it comes. They merely congratulate themselves for being so clever. If only they knew!

Great orators, painters, artists of all description, poets, writers, composers, even teachers, receive from their higher selves and when you are aware of it, when you cultivate it, when you open your heart and mind, then your intuition expands on many levels and many areas and aspects of your life. Whereby you can make a conscious effort to 'tune in' and you will find that inspiration comes to you without question. I suspect that, for many of you now, it seems to be spasmodic and tends to occur when you least expect it.

That is because you are only just beginning to tap its full potential. It is like a light trying to shine through in your world, into your life. But it can only do so through tiny cracks and sometimes you get a glimpse of it. But it is a very, very powerful force, for it is from your higher self. Trust to your intuition. Cultivate it, utilise it, use it and you will find that it will grow stronger and appear to become more reliable. In truth, it is always reliable because it is of the higher self. But it only appears sometimes to be unreliable because you are not used to dealing with it. When you understand it, and by that I mean you have to trust and to go with it and to allow it to express itself, it will show itself and prove itself to be very, very infallible. Perhaps this has provided some intuition and guidance for you."

Chapter Ten

For every Question, an Answer

White Feather has often commented that his work is 'touching souls' and this is never more in evidence than when he is engaged in answering questions. Both this, and the following chapter are devoted to some of the many questions to which the spirit sage has responded during public demonstrations:

Q: "When seeking a spiritual tutor, what are the qualities and in what order should we look for?"

White Feather: "What do you mean by a spiritual tutor?"

Questioner: "Someone who has, in your own opinion, something from which you can learn and progress."

White Feather: "Well let me refer you to the words that I said in my talk to you, in that you can learn from all things. I have learned a great deal from a tree. I have learned a great deal from an insect. I have learned a great deal from a small child. I have learned a great deal from an animal. And very often you know, it is the little things in life that provide the biggest answers. It is the most insignificant of creatures that provide the greatest teachings for you. But if you are referring to one who can provide you guidance, one who can provide you with illumination, there are many souls in your world who are doing this, because they are operating as instruments of the spirit. I would not recommend one, or another, because all service is service . There is no high or low, great or small. There are all those who serve the spirit and you can learn from all souls and all things. But you know, the greatest teacher of all lies within here [*The guide pointed at his chest*] because truth lies within and if you can attune with your innermost self, with your highest self, with your soul, you will find a truth that is beyond words, a truth that is beyond description. A truth that is truly from the higher aspects of the spirit."

Q: "Referring to the question of the termination of life, what about the subject of euthanasia, where individuals take or are helped to take their own lives because they can no longer live with pain or suffering?"

White Feather: "Let me say again, that I respect and understand the motive. When the physical body is in terminal decline and there is great pain and suffering and difficulty, naturally the one who is in the midst of it wants nothing more than to be withdrawn from it. And those who surround that loved one are often the ones who suffer even more, because of their compassion, because of their love, because they wish to alleviate that pain and take the suffering away. And that is often why the motive behind euthanasia is one which I can understand.

But let me say again that the law is the law, and in my understanding it is not right to take life. Those who do so must pay the consequences, whether it is in ignorance or whether it is in understanding. They must face the consequences of their actions.

Now I am not suggesting in any way that there is a judgmental deity who condemns them for it. But you must understand that every act is judged by its merits and by the level of awareness and spiritual understanding that has been reached.

But to answer your question simply, I am opposed to anything which takes life before the natural span of life is completed, if it is a wilful act."

Q: "Carrying on from that, would you consider that it is also wrong to prolong life with automatic machines and so on, when someone's time has come?"

White Feather: "Absolutely not, absolutely not. And let me refer you again to what I said earlier; that you cannot prolong life beyond that time when the soul is ready to leave, even though often it appears that you can. But there are numerous instances where all the life support machines and equipment and doctors and nurses and surgeons have done everything they can, and the soul still withdraws from the body. You see, all that is happening with your life support machines is that they are keeping the physical functions continuing to the point where the spirit can continue to manifest through it, if it chooses to do so. But that will only be able to continue until the point that the spirit withdraws because its life span upon your earth has been completed. When that time is reached, no doctor or surgeon, nurse or anyone in your world can prevent it. It is an impossibility. Do you understand that?"

Questioner: "Yes, thank you."

Q: "Could you please enlighten us on the power of prayer, particularly when we ask for forgiveness for our sins, and also in the concept of absent healing?"

White Feather: "I am a great advocate of prayer, because prayer is a thought energy and provided it is expressed from the heart, not the mere repetition of words that is so endemic in your religious institutions, then it contains a great power and vitality from within the soul. It reaches out not only to the one to whom it is directed in love, but also into the higher realms of my world where it is met by those souls who will reciprocate, who will be drawn to you and who will seek to answer your prayer in a way that is right for you. Not necessarily the way that you would wish, but a way that is beneficial to your soul. That is what you must understand.

As regarding forgiveness, whilst it is good to ask for forgiveness, it is again, the motive that is behind it. If there is a sincere desire for repentance, if there is a sincere desire that an individual should correct the imbalance which he or she has accrued through actions or thoughts or deeds, then that is to be commended. But in no way does that absolve you of the operation of natural law.

It is all very well you know, the priest standing at the bedside and making some sign or other and absolving you of your sins. That does not have any effect upon your soul at all. What you sow, you reap, and that which you do is that which you create. What you are today is that which you were, through your thoughts and deeds, yesterday. And that which you will be tomorrow is occurring through your creation today. But where there is a genuine desire, through prayer, for help and guidance and forgiveness, where there is a turning of the elements of that soul and it begins to awaken from its slumber, to reach out to the highermost, innermost realms of my world....and always, always, always there is a response from my world to such a soul. No one, however low they have sunk is left unattended, overlooked, forgotten or pushed to one side. Even in the lowest of the low there is the divine spark of the spirit. Has that helped you?"

Questioner: "Yes, thank you very much."

After enquiring whether everyone was 'enjoying themselves', the guide then took a question from a member of the audience who wanted to know when man's continuing destruction of his environment would come to an end?

White Feather: "That is a question which I ask myself frequently. You see, we cannot interfere with man's freewill and it is, that if man creates this within his mind, then what he creates as a thought, he also then manifests. Everything that you see around you is a manifestation of man's thinking, at some point. And everything which you are now witnessing, in terms of global destruction and pollution, is as a result of ignorant minds who have no true knowledge and understanding of the devastation which they are helping to manifest, which they are actually bringing into being. As to when it will end, it will end when there is knowledge, when there is understanding, when there is awareness of the true principles of natural law and especially when there is a recognition that what an individual does to others, he does to himself. When that dawns, and when that day comes when there is a deepening of man's awareness, when there is a recognition of his oneness with all of life, with every facet of creation, then there will be a turning of the tides and gradually, a greater perception and understanding will dawn.

That is why those of you who are here in this of your gathering this week are playing a great part. You should not in any way diminish what you are doing here. It is vital that you do this because this work you know, is like the arteries of the great body of the spirit truth that seeks to express itself, and you are the conduits, you are the veins and the arteries through which this truth can pour. It is only by changing the sum total of the parts that you affect the whole. So each of you can play your part.

Remember also this, and I have said this before too; that your world will never be a Garden of Eden, it will never be a paradise, it will never be a heaven on earth, because that is not the true purpose of this place. Even though we earnestly desire and seek and work to raise the level of consciousness and vibration to enable man to experience life in a more beautiful fashion, there will always be, upon this plane of opposites, difficulty and darkness that obtain, because it is here that the soul learns. That is the nature of physical experience. To facilitate the soul with the greatest possible discipline that can only be obtained by passing through difficulty, through darkness and light, negative and positive, male and female, ignorance and truth, freedom and captivity. That is what the earth plane teaches you. Do you understand that?"

The questioner answered in the affirmative, much to the satisfaction of the guide, before the session continued with an enquiry about the length of time it took for White Feather to master the art of linking with his medium:

White Feather: "It has taken a long time in terms of years, yes, because I was unable to link in the way, the fashion, that you now witness until this instrument had achieved adulthood. Although I did link with him before he entered into this body and I did work with him through his childhood, although his was unaware of my presence.

But there was a certain amount of guidance shall I say, on my part, and this was necessary to facilitate the very fine adjustment in attunement that is absolutely necessary to communicate in this way. And I had to wait for the opportunity, and even then it took me several years to establish what I regard as a sufficiently acceptable level of communication.

It is still an ongoing process, because in my view there is no such animal as a developed medium. Always the link has to be re-evaluated, re-estimated, re-honed, and this is as it should be because all progress is an ongoing thing."

Q: "Can you tell me if will you be speaking through this channel for the rest of his life?"

White Feather: "As long as I am able to maintain a link, and there are many factors of course, which determine that. Not least of which is the health and well being of the instrument, but also of course his thoughts, morals and other contributory factors. But it is my intention, yes. I am not planning on retiring yet!"

Q: "Will you please tell us how you see us. Do you see us as people sitting here, or as lights, or what?"

White Feather: "It depends. You know sometimes that varies, it fluctuates depending upon the level of control that I either choose to obtain or that is made available to me. But I see you as spirits. I see your spiritual bodies, I see your etheric bodies and in that sense they are filled with light. And that is the aspect which concerns me because I look not at the colour of your skin or your gender. I take into consideration your soul. That is what matters."

Q: "What is the most delightful thing about being involved in what you are doing with your instrument?"

White Feather: "Touching souls. There is nothing more wondrous than to touch a soul who is crying out for help. Perhaps one who is in the midst of turmoil or pain. It is beyond measure. It is priceless. For when you can awaken a soul, when you can touch a soul as you also have been doing, then you will find that the reward is beyond description. Because when a soul comes into a realisation then it is able to awaken from its slumber and begin to awaken all the richness and beauty that is inherent within, and that to me is beyond any measure. It is beyond description."

Once questions have been asked of the spirit guide, particularly during a public demonstration, it quite often occurs that those who had no initial intention of asking a question, actually do so. White Feather has a way of treating each questioner and every question with the utmost importance and respect, and this in itself often brings about an atmosphere which is conducive to learning. Here, the guide continues answering each question put to him without a moment's hesitation:

Q: "I have a question on healing. What is the advantage of having trance control in healing over ordinary contact healing?"

White Feather: "It depends upon the kind of healing to be administered but I believe, it is within my understanding, that where there is a greater degree of control then a greater power can often be put through that channel, through that instrument. But let me say that there are a great many healers, there are a great many instruments that can be used in their own unique ways. Sometimes through what you call absent healing, sometimes through what you term contact healing, and each is used in accordance with their constitution, with their ability to attune and their ability to link with our world.

Do not think in terms of high and low or greater and lesser because service is service and wherever there is healing put through an instrument in your world, whatever level of healing is achieved, it is always worthwhile because souls are being touched.

But in answer to your question; yes, where there is a deeper control and a greater linking with my world then by necessity all manner of healing can be put through in a far more potent and powerful way. Do you understand this?"

Questioner: "Yes I do."

White Feather: "That applies of course to all levels of mediumistic communication. Where there is a deeper control, there you have more of the spirit and less of the human."

The popular concept of an 'earth spirit', often referred to as Gaia, is something over which many people have pondered. It was interesting to hear the spirit teacher's views on the subject when asked the question during a public demonstration at the Arthur Findlay College:

Q: "I would ask if you can tell us about the spirit of the earth, particularly with all the damage being done by man?"

White Feather: "Let me say that this may not agree with your own concept, but the Great Spirit is to be found within every facet of life. The earth is not an individualised spirit, as is often thought. This was conceived by the mind of man. But nevertheless the earth has its spiritual aspect and if you look at it in that way, if you view it and understand it in that way then you are right in being concerned about the spirit of the earth. Because what man does to the body of matter, what he does to the earth has its effect upon the spirit. What you do to the body of matter affects the spirit and what affects the spirit affects the body of matter. So man must learn to have compassion and respect, understanding and tolerance for all life whether it is human, nature, animal, vegetable, mineral.....it is all part of the same scheme and what he does to the earth he does to himself."

At this point a question was raised concerning the use of colour in our day to day lives. White Feather, after first adding a touch of humour to the proceedings, which he often does to lift the vibrational energies, then proceeded to give an answer which may well interest those involved in the health professions:

Q: "I have a question about colour. In our present day we notice colour. In years gone by people didn't have access to colour in their lives, they were perhaps very poor. Is this part of our spiritual awakening, to be more aware of colour and use of colour?"

White Feather: "Have I answered this question before?"

Questioner: "Yes."

White Feather: "Then you know the answer!"

Questioner: "But I thought everybody else might like to know!"

White Feather: "For those who do not know the answer let me say of course you are becoming more aware in your world, of colour, as you are beginning to awaken to what you term 'complimentary therapies' and teachings as they become more acceptable to the consciousness of humanity. And as they become more mainstream, to use your terminology, then there is an awakening to the possibilities of their use in healing, and colour is a very, very powerful tool that can be used in conjunction with sound of which it is also a part.

For where there is colour there is sound. Where there is sound there is colour. And within your hospitals you will find an increased use of colour healing, sound healing, and as your regimented views of your health service and your doctors, surgeons and nurses begins to awaken and unfold you will find that there is a greater influx of these complimentary therapies that will bring great benefits to humanity. And never underestimate the power of colour.

You know, colours that you adorn yourselves with, the colours that you wear, each has an impact upon your mood and your well being. For example, if you are feeling depressed you should uplift yourselves with the bright colours; the yellows, the golds. If you are feverish then choose the coolness of the blue or the violet. If you are cold then choose the warmth of the red or the orange and these things will help you to provide a balance for the   condition with which you are affected. More understanding of colour will, I believe be of great benefit to humanity."

Chapter Eleven

Enquiring Minds

By far the most engaging aspect of White Feather's demonstrations are the question and answer sessions where the spirit teacher excels in his ability to tackle all manner of philosophical questions. Here are some more, beginning with one concerning the purpose of spirit communication:

Q: "What would you consider is the prime purpose of your communication with this world?"

White Feather: "Once again, it is to touch souls. It is to awaken, to inspire, to uplift. You know, your world is filled with many minds who are in ignorance, and ignorance breeds ignorance. If you have ignorance, then ignorance sows ignorance and what is sown must be reaped. We are facing a constant battle, a constant fight with the lower mind of man. Not with the devil, because the devil doesn't exist. Not with evil, except evil within men's minds. We are constantly having to oppose this. It is like a cancer that grows at the heart of humanity, that seeks to stifle and suffocate any vestige of spiritual light and verity. So we are always having to strive through the instruments available to us, to touch souls and awaken souls. Because only when you touch the parts can you affect the whole.

This is my work. I come to link with you as a teacher. Others link as healers, although I like to think that what I give you or teach you is itself, healing. But others are healers, others are message bringers, each has their own part to play. But for me, it is touching souls."

Q: "You have spoken about colour as being powerful, what is your view of crystals?"

White Feather: "Everything of that nature has it's aspect to be considered. Crystals are great magnifiers of energy. You can put energy into a crystal, you can release energy from a crystal, it can absorb toxins, it can help to magnify any energies, the magnetic energies with which you work. So they have many aspects which can be considered and are being considered, as man's awakening intellect and understanding unfolds. So I would never discard anything like that.

What I would say to you however, is that you must always keep a sense of balance. Within this which you call your 'New Age' there are a lot of things which, quite frankly, are nonsense and which you have to learn to disregard. You have to separate the wheat from the chaff, the gold from the dross, and it is a matter for your consideration, for your attunement as to what is right and what is not."

After commenting that the audience were 'working very well' White Feather went on to answer more in-depth questions from all parts of the auditorium, beginning with one concerning whether there was more than one spirit world, which brought a humourous response from the spirit teacher:

Q: "If there is intelligent life on other planets do they also have a spirit world?"

White Feather: "You know I sometimes wonder whether there is intelligent life on this world! There is but one spirit world and it has many expressions. There is not one planet within the universe that does not have its spiritual aspect. In reality, it is truth that will reveal this to you when you come into an understanding of it, but do not think of anything that is separated or segregated. All of life is one great ocean and the spirit world exists within the whole of being. Do you understand that?"

Questioner: "Yes........and if the population of this earth planet is always increasing does that mean to say that the spirit world is also increasing?"

White Feather: "Not necessarily, although let me assure you that we have ample room for everyone! But you must understand that there is a flow of individualised spirit souls who are manifesting into your world of matter and then withdrawing when death occurs. You know, it does not always follow that there is an increase in my world although I must admit that this is a general trend. But you must understand that many who were upon your earth, perhaps many millennia ago - the caveman for example, no longer have an expression in my world because the spirit that manifested aeons of time ago has since moved on, has come through other forms perhaps, many lifetimes since, upon your world, and continues to exist. Do you understand? You see, bodies here upon the earth are unique to this lifetime. Even though you continue to be the same person when you pass into my world you will not hold that form for all eternity and when you reincarnate it may be that, that form which was held for a while - perhaps a hundred....two hundred....three hundred years, no longer has a need to be held. So it dissolves. Do you understand that?"

Questioner: "Yes, thank you."

White Feather: "It is a very, very deep question in actual fact."

Q: "I've heard you speak so often about 'the soul', could you explain a little more about the soul please, and the difference between the mind and the soul?"

White Feather: "To me, the soul is the Great Spirit within, which in humanity is individualised. The mind is an aspect that the soul manifests through to gain expression, intellect, awareness, and in truth you will find that where there is the soul there is also mind. Where there is mind, you will find that there is the soul aspect also, because they are parts of one another. The difficulty here is one of semantics, because these are words which are intangible, seeking to describe something which is beyond the confines of language. So there is always a difficulty which we encounter in this way. But to me, the soul is the Great Spirit within, which in humanity is individualised. That soul manifests itself through lower form, that has to work through mind which thinks and reasons and gives expression to the soul. Does that help you?"

Questioner: "Yes it does, thank you."

White Feather: "I hope it doesn't confuse the issue, because as I say, it is a problem of semantics. It is difficult to convey that which is beyond the limitations of earth in earthly terms."

As the questions continued to flow from the many present, it was clear that each answer given by the spirit teacher, itself provoked another question from the audience, something which is often a feature of White Feather's public demonstrations:

Q: "As the spirit evolves, does the spirit of animals also evolve?"

White Feather: "Only to a point. It is not the purpose of the Great Spirit that what you call the spirit of animals should evolve to a higher degree than humanity. You see, the Great Spirit has many, many manifestations and the spirit that now functions at the animal level will, at some point in its future, reach the level of humanity. You my friend, have been amongst the lower aspects of life upon this earth, as have you all. It is not YOU who have been the monkey or YOU who have been the ape, or YOU the bird or YOU the fish, but the SPIRIT that expresses itself through you. And as that spirit comes into form so it gains higher and higher expression until it reaches the level of humanity, which believe it or not is the highest form of expression upon your earth - although I sometimes doubt this! And here it individualises and that individual expression is maintained for all time, all eternity. It does not return to its former state. It keeps on, expressing itself, perhaps through other human vehicles, male or female, but always there is an upward progression.

An animal that has existed upon your world will continue to do so if it has maintained or established a link with a human, and then you will find that sometimes that quickens its progress and it will continue to maintain its individuality when it too, passes to my world. But that does not endure for all time, for that is not the plan of life. There will come a point when the spirit which manifested through that animal will again enter into the body of matter that is at a higher and finer expression."

Q: "You sometimes mention spirit and sometimes mention soul, can you differentiate between the two? Is there any difference?"

White Feather: "As I have already stated, and I refer to my previous answer, to me the soul and the spirit are the same but the soul is the Great Spirit within, that is individualised. Everything has spirit. Everything IS spirit. But when it individualises, as in the human condition, there a soul quality is established. You can think of a soul you know, if you want to think of it in tangible terms......something with which you can identify.......do not think of it as being up there [*the guide pointed his finger at the sky*] it is not like a balloon tied to the end of a piece of string......the soul is neither within, although it is within, it is not confined. You know I have heard your medical profession recently state that it is within the pineal gland although how they have arrived at this conclusion is beyond me.....but you must understand that the soul is neither within or without. You can think of the soul, if it helps you, as a diamond that has many facets, many sides, and it is this diamond which is you, the individual. Not you the personality, not you the man or woman, but you the individuality. And when you come into form it is a facet of the diamond that incarnates into matter. That takes upon itself, personality, that endures for a certain length of time before it is returned to the whole. And in the fullness of time every facet has experienced and the whole, which is the soul, has benefited as a result."

The next question, asked by the 'chair person' allowed the guide to display some more of his customary humour, as he had done so often in the past, to the delight of all those present:

Q: "It is said that we do have freewill, but on the other hand people say that 'if it is written, it will happen'. So how do you explain freewill within the personal plan for each individual? How does it work? If we operate too much freewill, do we not operate our plan? And if we allow our plan to operate, should we be operating a little bit more freewill? I don't understand how it works?"

White Feather: "Is that a question or an essay?"

Chairperson: "It is a question!"

White Feather: "Let me say, with respect, that the question is a very good one. Let me say that there is a limited freewill within an overall scheme of life. All things are known from a higher level and there are certain aspects, when you incarnate, that will, if the plan of life unfolds as it should, occur within that allotted span. But that does not rule out freewill. Because if freewill were to be disregarded or if it did not exist then that would suggest that all life is predetermined and that whatever you did or whatever you said or thought would make no difference to what happened and that, quite clearly cannot be so. Because if that were so then all manner of things would be happening in your world and no one would have to pay the consequences of them. So freewill is paramount in the expression of all life at whatever level. Although at the higher levels there is a greater expression of freewill than at the lower levels. The higher that you evolve the more that your freewill can express itself. But it is always a limited freewill. It is never totally free, you understand. It is always within the limitations and the confines of the form through which it comes and the constraints and the constrictions that are placed upon that form. You my friends, although you are striving to raise your consciousness to higher levels, you can only do so within the confines of the form through which you manifest. Through your intellect, through your conditioning. Because make no mistake, there is always conditioning at every level and you have to manifest through this. So this places limitations upon you but nevertheless you have a degree of freewill.

Where perhaps you may be referring to events that are foreseen, when you say that 'if one can see the future, how does this then fit in with the scheme of freewill?', it is all a matter, all a question of the levels of being and time. Because time upon this level, which is of a linear nature, is not the same as on the higher levels of my world where past, present and future can merge into one and what is to come can be seen, even though at your level it has yet to be determined by an individual. That may sound a contradiction and be difficult for you to comprehend, and I appreciate that, but it is nevertheless the truth."

Q: "Are we all reincarnated?"

White Feather: "Are you all reincarnated? It is not, as I have said - and I refer to my talk with you last night at your gathering, that reincarnation is a fact for everyone. Although I have not yet found one who has not been reincarnated at this level, because you cannot learn everything in one lifetime. There are some who make great strides and do not need the number of incarnations that others do.

If you are referring to the many who are gathered here today, let me say to you that in my understanding, each of you has had previous experiences here upon this earth, although of course that would not necessarily be made available to your consciousness at this moment in time."

Q: "The problem seems to be that there are so many so called 'religions' with people who have a long way to go to reach the highest levels of consciousness."

White Feather: "You have to learn to strip away all of the dross. You know there are so many minds in your world who think that they have the absolute truth. I am always a little concerned, when I hear someone say 'I have the truth, this is the truth', because it is not. It is only a facet of the truth, of the whole truth, and that must be the mentality that must be changed, not only within your world, but let me say also within your movement. Because you must learn that truth unfolds. As you approach it, you must do so with an open mind."

Q: "As you link with your instrument, do you yourself also receive help and guidance from others in your world?"

White Feather: "Yes, yes. Let me say that just as I link with this instrument or this channel to provide you with teachings, so I also link with higher minds than myself. It is like a waterfall, where one links with another and so we are able, through this chain to bring knowledge and teachings from even higher sources than the one through which I am able to manifest.

I am part of a group which you may have become aware of perhaps, which is termed 'The White Brotherhood'. There are many outlets, many aspects many minds that contribute to that pool of knowledge from which I am able to draw. It is not infinite, it is not a pool of absolute knowledge, but it is a pool of knowledge and experience nevertheless. And it is a reciprocal effect, tied in with the earth's orbit[1] and so those of a higher mind are able to convey these teachings from other levels."

Q: "Which is the best way of spiritual communication, thought or speech?"

White Feather: "All communication, in essence, is thought. Whatever is spoken has first to have been thought of at some level. So, in answer to your question, all communication begins with thought. Everything that you see around you, the chairs upon which you sit, the curtains, the building, the clothes you wear, everything has been thought of by someone in some way. And thought always proceeds and precludes speech and action and so it is a natural consequence of being. Let me say that in terms of spiritual communication, the key to communication is attunement, and also motive. If the motive is good, if it is selfless, if it is through a desire to serve and if you can achieve a level of attunement with those in my world who would work through you, whether that be ultimately through speech, or in another way, but work through you, initially through the thought energies, then that is to be commended. It is all about attunement and it is all about motive. That is what counts."

Q: "Much has been written and channelled about the ascension process, the shift of humanity's consciousness to a higher level. Could you comment on this please?"

White Feather: "All of life is an 'ascension process' as you call it. All of life

[1]. White Feather was using the term 'orbit' in a general sense, NOT referring to the ACTUAL earth orbit.

is a movement from the lower to the higher. There is nothing that is ever still, there is nothing that is bereft of movement and humanity is an expression of the spirit. It is the desire and the purpose of the spiritual plan that is forever unfolding to provide a movement from ignorance to truth that will enable every individual encompassed within the Great Spirit, both in an individual sense and collectively, to come into a state of awareness. That is an ongoing process and one that has been in a state of movement and continuity since life appeared upon your world and even before then.

There are times when there is a great movement forward and we stand back and look and we are pleased at the progress being made, but often you know, man seems to take one step forward and two steps backward. There have been epochs.....of periods in your world where certain civilisations have crumbled from within, due to corruption or fraud and the return to materialistic values. There is such a change going on in your world at the moment because man has become more and more reliant upon material values and principles, and this has resulted, and continues to result in great damage to your world, to your environment, and ultimately this will reflect upon humanity. There has to be a clearing away of the dross before the purified state of being can re-emerge.

Ascension, as you refer to it, is an ongoing process. It does not end at death. Your world will never be a Garden of Eden, it will never be a place of paradise. It will never be perfect, it is only a stepping stone to the higher state of being which ultimately exists in the higher realms of light in my world. Perfection is never reached, it is never attained. It is always being sought but it is the directive of humanity, individually and collectively to reach that Nirvana of spiritual awareness, ascension and unfoldment. As to when that will occur, it is difficult to say because as I have already stated, the tide ebbs and flows. But it is that even though there is, in many ways a return to materialistic values upon your world, there are still a great many souls such as some of you who are here tonight, who have begun this awakening process, and that can only be a good thing in my view."

Q: "Many people during a near death experience, encounter a tunnel of light. What is your interpretation and definition of it?"

White Feather: "Of course death in the purest sense of the word does not occur, but I know in the context to which you refer to it. When this transition occurs there is an exchange of energies at many levels, from the lower to the higher. From the etheric to the astral to the spiritual.

You may be aware that there is a cord that connects your lower and higher levels of being which is often referred to as the 'silver cord'. It is rather like the umbilical that joins you to your mother at birth when you enter into this world. Very often you know, what is experienced when the transition called death occurs, is a part of the consciousness which is withdrawing through the silver cord, from the lower to the higher. Very often this is represented in the mental state as a tunnel. It does not occur in this way for everyone but it is a frequent experience and that is why so many report it you know, particularly when through illness or operation of some kind, their consciousness leaves the body.

You must understand, as I am sure you do, that the higher self is the real self. The physical body is only animated by the spirit and when the spirit withdraws and when death occurs, the silver cord is severed, it is cut. When that happens there can be no return for the spirit to the body of matter. This tunnel as it appears, as I have said, is because of the energies which are taken up from the lower to the higher."

Q: "Have you any proof that Jesus, the Christ, was the Son of God and not the Son of Man?"

White Feather: "What you refer to as 'Jesus, the Christ', was not the Son of God. Sorry if that disappoints you at all but you must remember that God is not an individual. The Great Spirit is everything. You are all in a sense, the sons and daughters of God. If man chooses to elevate an individual to the status of such as the 'Son of God' that is man's choice and he must face the consequences of that. But you will find in the fullness of time that there will be a movement away from that limited intellect and view point, towards a greater understanding that you are all parts and all children of the Great Spirit."

After enquiring, as he often does, whether the audience were all happy, commenting with some joviality on how quiet many of them were, White Feather continued taking more questions, starting with one concerning world peace:

White Feather: "Are you ever going to see world peace? It will not be in your lifetime upon this earth, in this span. However, I wish that it were. Again you must recognise and understand that this world of yours, as wonderful as it is, will never be a perfect place. It will not be a Garden of Eden where all life and all souls intermingle and have the same level of awareness and understanding because that is not it's purpose.

You must recognise that here upon your earth there are many minds of different awarenesses. Different levels of intellect and spiritual evolvement and they do not always see eye to eye. So I am afraid it will be a long time before there is what you call 'world peace'. Only when man recognises that his brother is himself, that what he does to others, whether it be human life, physical, or plant life, or animal life, or whatever........that what he does to that which resides outside of his being, he does to that which resides inside his being. What he does to others, he does to himself. When that is recognised, that will be a great leap forward to a state of equilibrium that will see all the facets of creation in a more harmonious and attuned state with each other."

Q: "How do you define the Holy Spirit?"

White Feather: "To me there is the Great Spirit. Whether you wish to refer to that as 'holy', whatever that may mean to you or others I do not know. To me there is the Great Spirit who is sometimes referred to as God or whatever label is chosen to be placed upon it, but the Great Spirit IS, always has been and always will be.

The Great Spirit in essence, is the light, knowledge and wisdom and all encompassing love that created the boundless universe with it's myriad of form and it's many facets that manifest at all levels of being. That is the Great Spirit. It always was and always will be. You are a part of that as is all of creation and it always will be. Does that help you?"

Questioner: "Yes, thank you."

Q: "When man plays with genetics is that altering the basic life that was given us by the Great Spirit?"

White Feather: "Yes it is, and I must say that it is with great consternation that I and many in my world witness man tampering with the code of genetics. I know that sometimes the motive is good, in that it seeks to provide answers and solutions to age old situations that involve illness and a genetic disposition to a certain disease or condition, but all too often you know, it is inspired and motivated by commercial greed and commercial drives and much of the tampering that is going on will result in the creation of further disharmony and weaknesses that will occur, that will have direct results upon the crops that you grow and ultimately upon man's physical body.

You must understand that genetics is a state of evolution, that the DNA code, as it is referred to has evolved over many millions of years and is in such a state, because it is the natural state of evolution. When you tamper with nature you are playing with fire and man must reap the consequences of his actions."

Q: "When a human soul departs this earthly body does it ever come back and revert or does it always make progress?"

White Feather: "You come here time and time again. There are those in your world who do not accept the principles of reincarnation. There are even some in my world who do not accept it, but I have always maintained it is a fact because you cannot learn everything in one lifetime upon the earth and also while you are here, because you are imperfect as are we all, you stumble, you err, you fall, you make mistakes and you set into motion the operation of law which must outwork itself.

There are some things that cannot be balanced and corrected at the spiritual level but which have to be rectified at the physical level. So it is that an aspect of the soul, never the total aspect, but a facet of the soul has to return to the earth, through a different personality, perhaps through a different gender and always through a different vehicle in order to put right what it has done wrong. To correct the imbalance and to offer a service that perhaps it did not in a previous life. So you come here time and time again but it is not an endless process because ultimately all progress is an upward movement and will continue indefinitely in my world."

Q: "Can you explain please why a baby just touches the earth for a very short time or doesn't live at all?"

White Feather: "You must look with the eyes of the spirit, not with the eyes of matter. I will answer this question by referring to the previous question that I have just answered, that it may be necessary for that facet, that soul aspect that has come through that baby, through that child, to touch upon the earth for a few moments, perhaps even seconds or even days or weeks in order to complete the lesson it has come to learn.

Time does not mean a great deal. It is not the length of time that you are upon the earth, it is what is learned, what is undertaken during the time you are here and very often you know, I see that young children are born into your world with perhaps a deformity, without the gift of sight or hearing, or devoid of limbs and of course they have the sympathy that is duly theirs. But you must look at the greater picture, the wider whole, to understand why it is that soul has chosen to undergo that experience. You cannot know that without looking at the whole. It may be that in a previous existence that individual had undertaken some particular course of action that resulted in the Karmic law being activated. That means that, that soul must come again to put right what it did wrong or to redress the balance. So you have to look at the whole."

Q: "Do we ever share the same families in subsequent lives?"

White Feather: "You do, you do, because you must understand that even though personalities change, individuals are often linked together and where there is love, there is no separation. Those who you regard as your family, your husbands, your wives, your children, your parents......you may well have expressed upon the earth at a different time, through a previous existence with those individuals.

You may perhaps, if I can illustrate this in a more simplified manner, realise that those who are your children now may have been your parents in a past life. Where there is love there is often a desire for individuals to reincarnate collectively, to help each other, to support each other and also to work out sometimes what have been difficult relationships, to redress the balance. It all comes down to reincarnation and the law of Karma which I have previously referred to."

Q: "I have heard that two facets of the spiritual diamond can be on earth at the same time. Is this what they call twin souls?"

White Feather: "Yes it is possible, though it is very rare let me say. But it can be so if there is a particular reason and purpose behind it, perhaps a service to be rendered. It is possible, yes. You have heard correctly."

Q: "People refer to God as a man but does God have any gender at all?"

White Feather: "No. The Great Spirit is neither male or female, is not a man. The Great Spirit is neither male or female and yet encompasses aspects of both. You must understand that the Great Spirit is not confined to form. He is not confined to a physical body. You know, the mistake that many make is in taking literally the words that man has been created in the form of God. You must understand that is true, but THAT form is not a physical body, because spirit is formless, God is formless. God is beyond form.

There are those in the higher realms of my world who appear as light, as pure light and energy and love and understanding. They do not manifest at all through what is recognisably a form as you would understand it. They do not always appear to you in that way because it would be a great shock to humanity and of course, they often choose to maintain the form that they had upon the earth plane, and that is as it should be. But at the higher levels of being, spirit moves beyond form because form is a limitation upon the expression of the spirit. Certainly that which you call God, which I call the Great Spirit, does not have form that you would understand."

Q: "Are you obliged to reincarnate? In some books I have read there is a choice there."

White Feather: "No one forces you to. You are not obliged in that sense, that you are......that you HAVE to reincarnate. No one will make you do so. But there will come a recognition, there will come a time when you realise that further progression upward cannot be accomplished without reincarnation, particularly if there are certain aspects from a past existence which have to be addressed. If there are certain imbalances that have to be corrected then it may be that you have to return to that former place in a different body, in a different lifetime in order to correct that before progressing. There is no compulsion. It merely means that you cannot move forward into the realms of greater light and understanding until that has been cleared up."

Q: "Do we astral travel at night and if so why?"

White Feather: "You do as you call it 'astral travel' because when the sleep state occurs the consciousness which at the present moment is seated in your physical brain, which is not the mind - it is only the organ that the mind uses, transfers to the astral body. You are then able to express a degree of consciousness through that astral body which may take you to wherever it is appropriate for you to go. That may be another part of your world or it may be into a realm of my world, in which case you will learn in the sleep state. Some of you, you know, travel to the halls of learning, to the halls of music, to the great libraries in my world or simply to be with those who have gone before you upon the great journey of life, although you cannot remember this when you awaken.

Sometimes you do however, remember in the form of what you call a dream, which may be very vivid. In which case it is often a reflection of what has actually occurred. Sometimes however, it gets distorted because as I have previously said, the lesser cannot contain the greater and when that consciousness returns to the physical body, it is rather like re-entering into a funnel that gets narrower and narrower and so its expression becomes distorted and memory becomes distorted and it does not represent a true representation of what has occurred in the sleep state in the astral plane. It is somewhat fragmented, which is why when you wake up you say 'I have had a dream and I remember this', but it was a little bit difficult to remember all of it. It was not as clear as it should have been, but in all probability it was an experience in the astral plane, because each of you when you enter the sleep state are entering into the astral level of being."

Q: " Is there any best way of achieving enlightenment whilst we are on this plane?"

White Feather: "It is said that many pathways lead to one place and that is true. There are many ways to find enlightenment. One teacher may afford one way, another may state another. In my view, the best way and the purest way is through service. There are so many in your world who are in need of help. The enemies of the spirit are ignorance, greed, superstition, hatred, jealousy, darkness.....but the weapons you have are love, kindness, understanding, tolerance, gentleness, wisdom. When you enable these higher aspects of your being to function through you at this level then you are giving service.

Service you know, does not always mean standing in the spotlight. It can mean working in the stillness and the silence hidden away from the eyes of man in the sanctuary. It can mean just listening to someone without saying anything, just providing a listening ear. It can mean saying a kind word here, or touching someone in a gentle way to uplift them and guide them. It is in so many ways that service can be rendered. When you serve.....because service is the passport of the soul.....when you serve, your energies and vibrations are quickened and more of the spirit can express itself through you. So to answer your question, service is the coin of the spirit. It is the passport of the soul. Serve and you will be served. Give and you will be given unto."

At the end of the evening White Feather indicated that he enjoyed nothing more than to speak with souls that have a desire to learn and to understand, and that this filled his heart with joy. He finished with the following words:

"It is my prayer that the radiant light of the Great Spirit will reach into the dark recesses of your heart and your mind, to illuminate them from within.

May the power and the love of the Great Spirit be with you all until we meet again. God bless you."

Chapter Twelve

Know Thyself

One of the many enduring features of White Feather's oratory is his unswerving loyalty to spirit laws and his consistent belief in the absolute love and truth of the creator. He often speaks without pause or hesitation, his words tumbling forth like gleaming drops of water from an ever flowing fountain. As long as there are those who will listen and there are souls to be won over to the truth, the patient spirit sage is only too pleased to serve. Here, in an unbroken discourse, he returns to one of his favourite themes and treats those present to a lengthy address, commencing in typical style with a warm greeting to everyone assembled:

"May I greet you all with the divine love and radiant light of the Great Spirit. The energies are very powerful here this night which is beneficial both to myself and to those who stand by my side and I hope for you also. It is with great joy that I welcome this opportunity to speak with you, for it enables me as always not only to impart some knowledge and truth to you who are it's seekers, but also to demonstrate the wondrous spontaneity of spirit communication. For I can say categorically that as I link through this instrument neither I nor he have any prior knowledge of any questions which you may later be invited to ask. That is as it should be because you know, the greatest power, the greatest demonstration of the spirit power is spontaneity. For where there is rehearsal, where there is tension and anxiety and worry, then it is more difficult for us to obtain the correct control conditions through which we can allow the great power of the spirit to flow unimpeded and unhindered and unfettered into your world. Some of you I know, I have spoken to before, many of you I have not, so I feel it is my obligation to state to you at the commencement that who I am is of little consequence in terms of personality because it does not matter who or what I say I am, it is the message not the messenger that is of the greatest import. It is sufficient to say perhaps, that I am like you, human in every regard and respect. I have the same faculties as you possess; eyes with which to see, ears through which to hear, a body through which to communicate, a mouth through which to speak.

Like you I am human in every respect. Where we differ perhaps is in the degree of our understanding and the fact that I am, to all intents and purposes, dead! But of course I am dead only to your world, because death does not occur for anyone, EVER.

You are all parts of the same Great Spirit and you are all upon an infinite pathway of endless unfoldment and development, that will see each of you, regardless of your spiritual understanding, continue to exist in my world when death occurs, in an unbroken sequence. There will be no day of judgement. You will not go to sleep, awakening only when God calls you and then to decide whether you live eternally or are cast into oblivion.

You will continue to exist as you are now, with all your strengths, your weaknesses, all your virtues. All that you have ever done and said and been and are, will be yours and yours alone to take forth into my world. No one will judge you, for you will judge yourselves, critically, but with a kindliness that is a result of your higher mind. Your higher soul being knows you even better that you know yourself.

I would like to begin as I sometimes do with a question which I have asked on occasions before. 'Who are you?' Do you know who you are or are you aware just of that facet of your greater self which presents itself every morning when you look in the mirror. Some of you are male, others are female. Some of you are of a younger age than others in terms of your physical span and yet these things are not the real you. These aspects which present themselves to your vision and to your five physical senses represent only a small part of what is a greater whole.

You are not what you seem to be. If you are not what you seem to be, then what are you? From whence do you come and whence do you go? You must understand perhaps, to answer this question, there has to be an awareness of what the Great Spirit or God is, because you are a part of the Great Spirit. Try to understand that the Great Spirit has always been and will always be. The Great Spirit has no beginning and will have no ending. The Great Spirit has always been throughout eternity, throughout time immemorial.

I know not of beginnings or endings, only of commencements. You are part of the Great Spirit and thus you have always been. But you have not always enjoyed the same level of awareness and consciousness that you now exhibit. Try to understand that you were sent like a stone skimming across the waters of life, like a tiny seed sent forth from the Godhead. So you were sent into the worlds of matter in order to gain experience and thus enable the divine aspect within you, the divinity within you, to express and unfold itself. That latent divinity, that latent perfection which has yet to be realised. Try to understand that you come into matter in order that this can be awakened, but you do not start at the top. You do not commence at the zenith. You do not begin at the top of the mountain. You have to start at the bottom and you have to come through all forms. Through mineral, through atomic levels, through vegetable, through animal, through insect and ultimately to reach man, in which time and place you individualise for the first time and that individuality is maintained for all eternity.

When I say that you have come through the atom or through the stone or through the fish or the bird or the insect, it is not YOU who has done so, but the SPIRIT that now works through you, that now manifests through you. It is not YOU who have been the bird or YOU who have been the fish or YOU who have been the monkey, but the SPIRIT that works through you and at these levels it is very restricted in its expression. It cannot think, it cannot reason as you can. What does a fish know? What can it think and understand of what it is? How can a tree have the ability to know that it is a tree? It does not, because it does not have the physical apparatus that allows the spirit to work through it in the way that it can through humanity. But all of life is a progression. It is an upward unfoldment from the lower to the higher, from darkness to light, from captivity to freedom, from ignorance to truth. And so it comes time and time again into form, exhibiting each time through that form with all the restrictions that are placed upon it in order that it might quicken its vibration and so become more and more aware of the divinity within it, until it reaches the point where it comes into human form.

Here, it quickens to the point where it can reason, it can think for itself and it can ask the question 'Who am I? WHO AM I? Where have I come from and where do I go to?' And it is only a facet that comes into form.

Those of you who are of a religious mind may wish to reflect upon what the Nazarene said to you; that 'in God's house there are many mansions'. In the *soul* there are many mansions. There are many levels, many rooms. It is only one facet of the soul that comes into form. Only one facet of the diamond that expresses itself at any time through a physical form and the lesser cannot contain the greater.

You have a higher self that is as yet unexpressed. You may not be aware of it because in this heavy, gross field of material form and substance it denies you access to a degree. You forget who you are and from whence you come but there is still that golden thread that binds you to your higher self, to your soul and to all the knowledge and experience of many lifetimes that reside there. It is when you awaken that experience that you begin to allow this great potential to work through you and to bring you all manner of knowledge and truth and richness that even I cannot express in words.

You can think of it if you like, you can think of yourselves as being a tree. You have many levels. In the winter when the tree is dormant the sap is deep within the roots. What is above the ground seems to be dead. There are no leaves, no flowers, no fruit, no buds, and yet as the days lengthen and the air becomes warm and the temperature rises, so the sap begins to rise within the tree. The buds form and open. The flower appears. The leaves come into being and then the fruit, and the whole tree comes to life. So it is with you. That when through many lifetimes, through successive lifetimes, that encompass a multitude of experience, this panorama of experience, of light and dark, good and bad, high and low, male and female, it comes into this place of awakening and you become aware of your higher bodies, of your higher selves. For you have a physical body, you have an etheric body, you have an astral body, you have a mental body and you have a spirit body, and all of these are parts of what is the totality of yourself.

The more that you open up, the more that you awaken, the more that your vibrations quicken and you have access to these higher levels of your being. This is a wondrous thing. So when you begin to think of who you are, remember it is only a part of you that is expressing itself here now. You have come here time and time again. You know it is not an endless journey to the earth. You came because you have specific lessons to learn or a certain service to render and each time you come, because you are imperfect, you create through the laws of cause and effect, Karma, which has to be out-worked. For within every cause there is an effect and within each effect there is a cause and so it goes on. But you do not come here endlessly because the more that you evolve, the less that you err, the less mistakes that you make, the less that you stumble and fall. Eventually you will find that you come here and touch upon this world for the last time. Then you will continue your progress in my world, into the realms of light and unfoldment, as is your spiritual destiny.

So I would ask you to think upon these things. Remember that it is only a part that is expressing itself. It is not the totality. But you are not separate from my world. You are not separate from your soul and you are not separate from God. The Great Spirit is not an individualised deity, who sits upon a throne, awaiting a day of judgement, looking over his subjects. The Great Spirit is within everything that is, particularly within you as an individual, and it is that when that is awakened, all manner of beauty and richness can be yours. It is your pathway. It is your destiny. It is my purpose to help you, to guide you and to instruct you in that awakening. What I have to say to you is not a command. I do not dictate. My appeal is always directed to your reasoning mind and you, because you have freewill, because you have intelligence, are free to reject anything that I say to you. All that I ask is that you think about it first. If it finds a lodgement within your heart, then that is good. If you reject it, put it aside and let it be like a book upon a shelf gathering dust. Perhaps one day you will return to look within its pages. It is after all, only when the pupil is ready that the master appears."

Mere words do little justice to the love that is engendered by a communication from White Feather and on more than one occasion comment has been made by those present of the way in which the whole atmosphere within the room changes as he draws close. The language used, the vocabulary and the phraseology employed are beyond those of his medium and reflect, at least in part, the eloquence of a mind free from the constraints of an earthly body. For any earthly soul to consciously attempt to remember, without the aid of a script, an address which may last anything up to thirty minutes without pause, would be difficult in the extreme. That White Feather is a master of his subject seems almost beyond question, for he is never at a loss for words and demonstrates his understanding of truth in a way that is both simple and yet profound. Although he would refrain from speaking of his own abilities, out of a deep humility, it has to be said that he is both a wise teacher and a skilled diplomat. For his answers, although always faithful to the truth, are always carefully worded so as not to offend even the most ignorant of minds.
It is perhaps fitting then that we should leave these last few words to the spirit mentor, whilst looking forward to the time when we too can share in the same degree of understanding that he seeks always to impart to us:

"Take within yourselves the great reservoir of strength that is around you. Drink deeply of it. Let it fill every pore of your body. Let it fill every facet of your being. When others around you are fearful, when others around you are saying that man should fight man, brother should fight brother, when men speak of violent acts and crimes against their fellow man, realise that it is you who have this great responsibility. Because it is you who have knowledge of spiritual matters. Do not be fearful. Speak quietly and simply to state your case. Because it is you who are the mouthpieces of the Great Spirit. It is you who are the voices that cry out in the darkness and the wilderness. You may think that others do not listen, but the voice of the spirit will be heard. It WILL be heard.

Take strength my friends. Fear ye not. Harbour not fear nor worry for we know what awaits man. We know of his spiritual destiny. It is a future that is bathed in the sunlight of spiritual knowledge and truth. We know that each of you will climb this ladder because you cannot fail. Darkness there may be, difficulty and pain may be abundant around you, but you know yourselves that the flower of the spirit grows in the darkest wilderness. You look around you and you see in your concrete jungles the tiny flower that grows amidst the paving stones. Against all the odds it grows. The tiny flower that blooms in the darkness and that is not even seen, sometimes, by the eyes of man. And yet it is there, because you cannot prevent this great benign power from fulfilling its supreme purpose. There is perhaps, a little of which I have spoken from which you can take solace and comfort. But remember that there is no end to the pathway of learning upon which we all walk, myself included.

May the blessings of the Great Spirit touch deep within you and may their gentle embrace fill you with joy and vigour and strength for the days that lie ahead."

Visit the White Feather web site:
http://web.ukonline.co.uk/mandrob